IMPACT IMPRESS

RHETORICAL DEVICES FOR HEARTS AND MINDS

NILAM PATHAK

To our Parents

Contents

Contents

Contents

Preface

Rhetoric is the art of influence or impactful speaking or writing and is utilized to persuade, inform or motivate audience in a particular situation. Rhetoric is considered as one of the ancient art of discourse, along with logic and grammar. It improves the facility of speakers or writers with the exploitation of figures of speech and other language compositional techniques. For millenniums it has played a central part in western tradition and has been the subject of formal study and productive civic practice. Aristotle defines rhetoric best by calling it "the faculty of observing in any given case the available means of persuasion."

Rhetoric provides a set of rules for discovering, understanding and developing arguments in specific situations including logos, pathos and ethos, which are described by Aristotle as necessary elements for persuasive appeals. A persuasive speech requires invention, arrangement, style, memory and delivery. Western writers and speakers have used it for centuries to influence audience and to motivate them for action.

Rhetoric can be used as a tool to create impact in our writing and speaking. Its goal is to persuade, create impression and interest in the discussion. The study of rhetoric is required to understand the technicalities of the speech to make it highly persuasive for the reader or listener. This study would guide us to create the magic every time we communicate. We can use this understanding to carefully develop and deliver our effective communication instead of learning the hard-way, using hit and trial.

Good communication is much more than words and sentences written or spoken by writers or speakers as this communication has to be received and comprehended by other person, who has different understanding and perception of the world and events. To create the required rhetorical impact on readers and listeners the communication needs to be clear, interesting, unique and memorable. This type of communication is generally persuasive and convincing. In addition to logical points, supporting proofs an effective delivery requires style; rhetoric brings that style.

Prologue

Rhetorical Devices

In rhetoric, a rhetorical device or resource of language is a technique that an author or speaker uses to convey to the listener or reader a meaning with the goal of persuading him or her towards considering a topic from a different perspective.

While rhetorical devices may be used to evoke an emotional response in the audience, there are other reasons to use them. The goal of rhetoric is to persuade the subject towards a particular frame of view or a specific course of action, so appropriate rhetorical devices are used to construct sentences designed both to make the audience receptive through emotional changes and to provide a rational argument for a specific perception or direction.

There are large numbers of rhetorical devices but only certain rhetorical devices are required for effective communication. These devices are frequently used by politicians in their speeches or business executives in their presentations to persuade the listeners for their case. The master of these devices is able to create a magical influence on the mind of the receiver. This book aims to equip the readers with 63 of these rhetorical devices which can be used to get success in life.

The theme of this book is kept extremely simple. For each of the device a brief description is presented, followed by various examples. Readers can understand the concept and should use these devices in their daily communication to get mastery. It is important to understand that the specified rhetorical devices should be used strategically and optimally, as excessive use would blunt their impact.

CHAPTER ONE

Rhetorical Device 1 – Alliteration

Alliteration is used to create rhetorical impact through repetition of same sounds or the same kinds of sounds at the start of the words or in the stressed syllables, beginning either with a consonant or a vowel, in close succession. This can be used in clauses, phrases or sentences.

Two kinds may be distinguished:

1) Immediate juxtaposition occurs when the second consonant sound follows right after the first -- back-to-back.

2) Non-immediate juxtaposition occurs when the consonants occur in nonadjacent words.

<u>**Examples**</u>

<u>Brand Names</u>

- Dunkin' Donuts
- PayPal
- Best Buy
- Coca-Cola
- Park Place
- American Apparel
- American Airlines
- Chuckee Cheese's
- Bed Bath & Beyond
- Krispy Kreme

- The Scotch and Sirloin

<u>Names</u>

- Ronald Reagan
- Sammy Sosa
- Jesse Jackson
- Michael Moore
- William Wordsworth
- Mickey Mouse
- Porky Pig
- Lois Lane
- Marilyn Monroe
- Fred Flintstone
- Donald Duck
- Seattle Seahawks

<u>Phrases and Quotes</u>

- Busy as a bee
- Get your goat
- Good as gold
- Home sweet home
- Last laugh
- Leave in the lurch
- Living the life
- Look to your laurels
- Make a mountain out of a molehill
- Method to the madness
- Moaning Minnie
- Out of order
- Pleased as punch
- Pooh-pooh

<u>Other Examples</u>

- Annie's aunt ate apples and acorns around august.
- Betty's beagle barked and bayed, becoming bothersome for Billy.
- Cory collected cola cans counting continuously.
- They felt dreary and dismal in the darkness of the night.
- Dan's dog dove deep in the dam, drinking dirty water as he dove.
- Eric's eagle eats eggs, enjoying each episode of eating.
- Hannah's home has heat hopefully.
- Sara's seven sisters slept soundly in sand.
- Walter walked wearily while wondering where Wally was.
- Xavier's x-rayed his xylophone.
- Yarvis yanked you at yoga, and Yvonne yelled.
- Zachary zeroed in on zoo keeping.
- "I think a need a bigger box." – (*Taco Bell Commercial*)
- "No one standing in this house today can pass a puritanical test of purity that some are demanding that our elected leaders take." – (*Richard Gephardt*)
- "Isn't that what being an international man of mystery is all about?"-- (*Delivered by Mike Myers from the movie Austin Powers: International Man of Mystery*)
- "Was he not unmistakably a little man? A creature of the petty rake-off, pocketed with a petty joke in private and denied with the stainless platitudes in his public utterances."-- (*C.S. Lewis The Screwtape Letters*)
- "This generation of soldiers, sailors, airmen, Marines, and Coast Guardsmen have volunteered in the time of certain danger. They are part of the finest fighting force that the world has ever known. They have served tour after tour of duty in distant, different, and difficult places...They are men and women -- white, black, and brown -- of all faiths and all stations -- all Americans, serving together to protect our people, while giving others half a world away the chance to lead a better life....In today's wars, there's not always a simple ceremony that signals our troops' success -- no surrender papers to be signed, or

capital to be claimed...."-- *(Barack Obama, Fort Hood Memorial Service Speec)*

- "With a determination for an execution consistent with our record, squaring our performances with our promises, we will proceed to the fulfillment of the Party's mission. God helping, it shall be accomplished." -- *(Will H. Hays)*
- "Have you forgotten you're facing the single finest fighting force ever assembled?"-- *(Delivered by Dan Ackroyd from the movie Dragnet)*
- "We can no longer afford to traffic in lies or fear or hate. It is the poison that we must purge from our politics, the wall that we must tear down before the hour grows too late. But if changing our hearts and our minds is the first critical step, we cannot stop there. It's not enough to bemoan the plight of the poor in this country and remain unwilling to push our elected officials to provide the resources to fix our schools."-- *(Barack Obama, Address at Ebenezer Baptist Church)*
- "Somewhere at this very moment a child is being born in America. Let it be our cause to give that child a happy home, a healthy family, and a hopeful future."-- *(Bill Clinton, 1992 Democratic National Convention Acceptance Address)*
- "And our nation itself is testimony to the love our veterans have had for it and for us. All for which America stands is safe today because brave men and women have been ready to face the fire at freedom's front."-- *(Ronald Reagan, Vietnam Veterans Memorial Address)*

CHAPTER TWO

Rhetorical Device 2 – Allusion

Allusion is utilized to create rhetorical impact through a brief, indirect and casual reference to a place, person, thing or idea of historical, cultural, literary or political significance or work of art. It is to be noted that the specified referent of an allusion should be well known to the readers or listeners as it does not describe in detail the person or thing to which it refers.

Allusion is like a spontaneous comment and the speaker expects the listeners (or writer expects the readers) to possess enough knowledge to identity the allusion and absorb its importance in the sentence. Sources to the allusion may include religious texts, myths, history, events, popular celebrities, media content etc.

<u>**Examples**</u>

- Henry Ford of the Biotech Century
- "The killer wore a mark of Cain as he stalked his brother" – *(refers to the Biblical story of Cain and Abel)*
- "He was a Good Samaritan yesterday when he helped the lady start her car." *(This refers to the biblical story of the Good Samaritan)*
- "She turned the other cheek after she was cheated out of a promotion." *(This comes from teaching of Jesus that you should not get revenge)*

- "This place is like a Garden of Eden." (*The Garden of Eden was the paradise God made for Adam and Eve*)
- "She was breathtakingly beautiful, but he knew that she was forbidden fruit." (*This is an example of an allusion in the story of Genesis of the Holy Bible*)
- "You are a Solomon when it comes to making decisions." (*This refers to King Solomon, who was very wise*)
- "When the volcano erupted, the nearby forest was swallowed up in dust and ash like Jonah." (*Jonah was a person who was swallowed alive by a whale*)
- "It is raining so hard, I hope it doesn't rain for 40 days and 40 nights." (*This makes a reference to the biblical story of Noah and the ark he built. He was told by God that it would rain for 40 days and 40 nights and flood the land*)
- 'The earth was all before me', the fourteenth line of The Prelude written by William Wordsworth, alludes to the final phrases of Paradise Lost by John Milton: "The world was all before them". It is believed that Paradise Lost also refers to the story of Adam and Eve in Genesis.
- "I was surprised his nose was not growing like Pinocchio's." This refers to the story of Pinocchio, where his nose grew whenever he told a lie. It is from The Adventures of Pinocchio, written by Carlo Collodi.
- "I was not born in a manger. I was actually born on Krypton and sent here by my father, Jor-el, to save the Planet Earth." *-- (Senator Barack Obama, speech at a fundraiser for Catholic charities, October 16, 2008. In this statement, it is very apparent that Barack Obama is making a direct reference to Jesus Christ, who was born in a manger, and the very popular Superman, a superhero created by DC Comics and born on Krypton*)
- "When she lost her job, she acted like a Scrooge, and refused to buy anything that wasn't necessary." (*Scrooge was an extremely stingy character from Charles Dickens', A Christmas Carol*)
- "I thought the software would be useful, but it was a Trojan Horse." (*This refers to the horse that the Greeks built that*

contained all the soldiers. It was given as a gift to the enemy during the Trojan War and, once inside the enemy's walls, the soldiers broke out. By using trickery, the Greeks won the war)

- "I violated the Noah rule: predicting rain doesn't count; building arks does." *(Here, Warren Buffet is citing the idea of Noah, from the Bible, preparing for the great flood that was to arrive)*

- "He was a real Romeo with the ladies." *(Romeo was a character in Shakespeare's play, Romeo and Juliet, and was very romantic in expressing his love for Juliet)*

- "Chocolate was her Achilles' heel." *(This means that her weakness was her love of chocolate. Achilles is a character in Greek mythology who was invincible. His mother dipped him in magical water when he was a baby, and she held him by the heel. The magic protected him all over, except for his heel)*

- "And I can pledge our nation to a goal: When we see that **wounded traveler on the road to Jericho**, we will not pass to the other side."-- *(George W. Bush, 2000 Inaugural Address)*

CHAPTER THREE

Rhetorical Device 3 – Amplification

Amplification is a commonly used rhetorical device to emphasize a specific word or expression by attaching details to it, sometimes extensively. This device allows the speaker or writer to focus the attention of the listeners or readers to a word or idea, so that its importance can be highlighted and impact can be created.

Examples

- **Blackadder's Crisis**: "This is a crisis. A large crisis. In fact, if you've got a moment, it's a twelve-story crisis with a magnificent entrance hall, carpeting throughout, 24-hour portage, and an enormous sign on the roof, saying 'This Is a Large Crisis.' A large crisis requires a large plan. Get me two pencils and a pair of underpants." -- *(Rowan Atkinson as Captain Blackadder in "Goodbyeee." Blackadder Goes Forth, 1989)*

- **Dickens on Newness** : "Mr. and Mrs. Veneering were bran-new people in a bran-new house in a bran-new quarter of London. Everything about the Veneerings was spick and span new. All their furniture was new, all their friends were new, all their servants were new, their place was new, . . . their harness was new, their horses were new, their pictures were new, they themselves were new, they were as newly-married as was lawfully compatible with their having a bran-new baby, and if they had set up a great-grandfather, he would have come home in matting from Pantechnicon, without a scratch upon him, French-polished to the crown of his head."-- *(Charles Dickens, Our Mutual Friend, 1864-65)*

- In my hunger after ten days of rigorous dieting I saw visions of ice cream--mountains of creamy, luscious ice cream, dripping with gooey syrup and calories.
- This orchard, this lovely, shady orchard, is the main reason I bought this property.
- . . . Even in Leonardo's time, there were certain obscure needs and patterns of the spirit, which could discover themselves only through less precise analogies--the analogies provided by stains on walls or the embers of a fire. – *(Kenneth Clark)*
- Pride--boundless pride--is the bane of civilization.
- He showed a rather simple taste, a taste for good art, good food, and good friends.

CHAPTER FOUR

Rhetorical Device 4 – Anacoluthon

The dictionary definition of Anacoluthon is "a construction involving a break in grammatical sequence", as it often contains a sentence interrupted halfway, which then has a change of form. Its objective is to create a rhetorical impact with an abrupt change within a sentence to a second construction, which is inconsistent with the first.

<u>Examples</u>

- Agreements entered into when three states of facts exists – are they to be maintained regardless of changing conditions? -- *(John George Diefenbaker)*
- Had ye been there – for what could that have done? -- *(John Milton in Lycidas)*
- "I will have such revenges on you both, That all the world shall-- I will do such things, What they are, yet I know not." -- *(William Shakespeare, King Lear)*
- "A plank that was dry was not disturbing the smell of burning and altogether there was the best kind of sitting there could never be all the edging that the largest chair was having." -- *(Gertrude Stein, "A Portrait of Mabel Dodge," 1912)*
- "John McCain's maverick position that he's in, that's really prompt up to and indicated by the supporters that he has." -- *(Sarah Palin, vice presidential debate, Oct. 2, 2008)*

- And then the deep rumble from the explosion began to shake the very bones of--no one had ever felt anything like it.
- Be careful with these two devices because improperly used they can--well, I have cautioned you enough.
- "Sleepy reporters commit anacoluthon in this kind of sentence: 'The patrolman said he had never seen "an accident so tragic in all his career."' The patrolman surely said 'my career.'" -- *(John B. Bremner, Words on Words. Columbia Univ. Press, 1980)*
- " . . . I could have brought him in his breakfast in bed with a bit of toast so long as I didn't do it on the knife for bad luck or if the woman was going her rounds with the watercress and something nice and tasty there are a few olives in the kitchen he might like I never could bear the look of them in Abrines I could do the criada the room looks all right since I changed it the other way you see something was telling me all the time I'd have to introduce myself not knowing me from Adam very funny wouldn't it . . ." -- *(From Molly Bloom's monologue in Chapter 18 of Ulysses by James Joyce)*

CHAPTER FIVE

Rhetorical Device 5 – Anadiplosis

Anadiplosis is used to create rhetorical impact through the repetition of word or se of words in successive phrases or sentences that the following phrase starts with the same word with which the previous phrase had ended. The objective is to emphasize on a specific word or set of words to bring them to the attention of the reader.

Examples

- The world just wants us **to fit in**, and **to fit in** we just gotta be like everybody else."
- "Fear leads to **anger. Anger** leads to **hate. Hate** leads to suffering." — (*Yoda, Star Wars*)
- "For Lycidas is **dead, dead** ere his prime, Young Lycidas and hath not left his peer." — (*John Milton, Lycidas*)
- "Tonight, we are a country awakened to danger and called to defend freedom. Our grief has turned to **anger**, and **anger** to resolution."-- (*George W. Bush, 9-20-01 Address to Congress and the Nation*)
- "Our doubt is our **passion**, and our **passion** is our task." – (*Henry James*)
- 'The land of my **fathers**. My **fathers** can have it.' – (*Dylan Thomas on 'Wales'*)

- "The love of wicked men converts to **fear**; That **fear** to **hate**, and **hate** turns one or both To worthy danger and deserved death." – (*Richard II by William Shakespeare*)
- 'Talent is an **adornment**, an **adornment** is also a concealment' – (*Nietzsche*)
- 'The poor wish to be **rich**, the **rich** wish to be happy, the single wish to be **married**, and the **married** wish to be dead.' – (*Ann Landers*)
- "Watch your thoughts; they become **words**. Watch your **words**; they become **actions**. Watch your **actions**; they become **habits**. Watch your **habits**; they become **character**. Watch your **character**; it becomes your destiny." (*Proverb, original source unknown*)
- "Queeg: 'Aboard my ship, excellent performance is **standard. Standard** performance is **sub-standard. Sub-standard** performance is not permitted to exist.'" — (*Herman Wouk, The Caine Mutiny*)
- "Mine be **thy love**, and **thy love**'s use their treasure." — (*Shakespeare, Sonnet 20*)
- "Having power makes [totalitarian leadership] **isolated; isolation** breeds **insecurity; insecurity** breeds **suspicion and fear; suspicion and fear** breed violence." — (*Zbigniew Brzezinski, The Permanent Purge: Politics in Soviet Totalitarianism*)
- "What I present here is **what I remember of the letter**, and **what I remember of the letter** I remember verbatim (including that awful French)." — (*Vladimir Nabokov, Lolita*)
- "Strength through **purity, purity** through faith." — (*Chancellor Adam Susan, V for Vendetta*)
- "Information is not **knowledge, knowledge** is not **wisdom, wisdom** is not **truth, truth** is not **beauty, beauty** is not **love, love** is not **music** and **music** is the best." – (*Frank Zappa*)
- "They call for you: The general who became a **slave**; the **slave** who became a **gladiator**; the **gladiator** who defied an Emperor. Striking story." —(*Commodus, Gladiator - 2000 film*)

- "Turn the lights out **now; Now** I'll take you by the **hand; Hand** you another **drink; Drink** it if you **can; Can** you spend a little **time; Time** is slipping **away; Away** from us so **stay; Stay** with me I can **make; Make** you glad you came" — (*Glad You Came by The Wanted*)

- "My father was very sure about certain matters pertaining to the universe. To him all good things -- trout as well as eternal salvation --come by **grace** and **grace** comes by **art** and **art** does not come easy." - (*Norman McLean, A River Runs Through It and Other Stories*)

- "Kinetic energy is also known as the **energy of motion**. A vehicle's **energy of motion** doubles when its **weight doubles**. When a vehicle's **weight doubles**, it needs about twice the distance to stop."

- "Of course our vision and our aims go far beyond the complex arguments of economics, but unless we get the economy right we shall deny our people the opportunity to share that vision and to see beyond the narrow horizons of economic necessity. **Without a healthy economy we can't have a healthy society** and **without a healthy society the economy won't stay healthy for long**." – (*Margaret Thatcher, The Lady's Not For Turning*)

- "Integrating our counterterrorism and regional strategies was the most difficult and the most important aspect of the new strategy to get right. Al-Qaida was both a client of and a patron to the Taliban, which in turn was supported by Pakistan. America's al-Qaida policy wasn't working because **our Afghanistan policy wasn't working**. And **our Afghanistan policy wasn't working** because our Pakistan policy wasn't working." – (*Condoleezza Rice, Statement to the 9/11 Commission*)

- "Once you change your philosophy, **you change your thought pattern**. Once **you change your thought pattern, you change your attitude**. Once **you change your attitude**, it changes your behavior pattern and then you go on into some action."-- (*Malcolm X, The Ballot or the Bullet*)

CHAPTER SIX

Rhetorical Device 6 – Analogy

Analogy is used to bring clarity in the minds of the subject (the target – listeners or readers) for a specific point or idea through an explicit comparison of two things based on their being alike in some way. It creates rhetorical impact by giving an idea of an inference or creating an image in the mind of listeners or readers for enhancing the reasoning.

<u>Examples</u>

- You are as annoying as nails on a chalkboard. (*A person must be pretty annoying for someone to say that*)
- I am going to be toast when I get home. (*This is usually said when someone is in trouble with their significant other*)
- He is like a rock. (*This means he is steadfast and strong*)
- I feel like a fish out of water. (*This implies that you are not comfortable in your surroundings*)
- She was as quiet as a mouse. (*This means she was very quiet*)
- Bing Crosby had a velvet voice. (*This implies that his voice was smooth and soothing*)
- Life is like a box of chocolates. (*Life is sweet*)

<u>Other Examples</u>

- Just as a caterpillar grows out of its cocoon, so we must grow out of our comfort zone.
- Obeying is to a servant, like ordering is to a master.
- Green is to go as red is to stop.
- Just as the earth revolves around the sun, an electron revolves around the nucleus.
- What a general is to an army, a CEO is to a company.
- Day is to month as minute is to hour.
- Small is to petite as large is to giant.
- Pencil is to write as crayon is to color.
- Pig is to pork as cow is to beef
- Word is to sentence as page is to book
- Plane is to hangar as car is to garage
- Pen is to author as brush is to artist.
- Just as sword is the weapon of a warrior, pen is the weapon of a writer.
- **"Our men in uniform are like the college football players.** While the struggle is impending, they are observing the rules of training that they may be fit to fight. But when the game has been won, the temptation to break training and make up for the restraints of the past months and years will be a mighty one." *(John D. Rockefeller, Jr., War Campaign Address)*
- "If you want my final opinion on the mystery of life and all that, I can give it to you in a nutshell. **The universe is like a safe** to which there is a combination. But the combination is locked up in the safe." *(Peter De Vries, Let Me Count the Ways. Little Brown, 1965)*
- "Dumb gorgeous people should not be allowed to use literature when competing in the pick-up pool. It's like **bald people wearing hats.**" *(Delivered by Matt McGrath (from the movie Broken Hearts Club)*
- "Don't worry about the future; or worry -- but know that worrying is as effective as trying to **solve an algebra equation by chewing bubble gum.**" *(Baz Luhrmann, Everybody's Free (to Wear Sunscreen)*

- "Remember this, ladies and gentlemen. It's an old phrase, basically anonymous -- that politicians are a lot like diapers: They should be changed frequently and for the same reason. Keep that in mind next time you vote. Good night." *(Delivered by Robin Williams from the movie Man of the Year)*
- "MTV is to music as KFC is to chicken." *(Lewis Black)*
- "Memory is to love what the saucer is to the cup." *(Elizabeth Bowen, The House in Paris, 1949)*
- "**Cameron's house is like a museum**. It's very cold, and very beautiful, and you're not allowed to touch anything." *(Matthew Broderick as Ferris in Ferris Bueller's Day Off, 1986)*
- "If I had not agreed to review this book, I would have stopped after five pages. After 600, I felt as if **I were inside a bass drum banged on by a clown**." *(Richard Brookhiser, "Land Grab." The New York Times, Aug. 12, 2007)*
- "Withdrawal of U.S. troops will become like salted peanuts to the American public; the more U.S. troops come home, the more will be demanded." *(Henry Kissinger, Memo to President Richard Nixon, 10 September 1969.*

CHAPTER SEVEN

Rhetorical Device 7 – Anaphora

Anaphora is used to create rhetorical impact through the deliberate repetition of a word, a set of words or phrase at the beginning of successive verses, clauses, sentences or paragraphs. The objective is to put stress on a specific word, phrase or clause to create a rhythm, making it more impactful and memorable.

Examples

- "**I needed** a drink, **I needed** a lot of life insurance, **I needed** a vacation, **I needed** a home in the country. What I had was a coat, a hat and a gun." *(Raymond Chandler, Farewell, My Lovely, 1940)*
- "**I don't** like you sucking around, bothering our citizens, Lebowski. **I don't** like your jerk-off name. **I don't** like your jerk-off face. **I don't** like your jerk-off behavior, and **I don't** like you, jerk-off."-- *(Policeman in The Big Lebowski, 1998)*
- "Sir Walter Raleigh. **Good** food. **Good** cheer. **Good** times."-- *(Slogan of the Sir Walter Raleigh Inn Restaurant, Maryland)*
- "**We saw** the bruised children of these fathers clump onto our school bus, **we saw** the abandoned children huddle in the pews at church, **we saw** the stunned and battered mothers begging for help at our doors."-- *(Scott Russell Sanders, "Under the Influence," 1989)*
- "Of **all** the gin joints in **all** the towns in **all** the world, she walks into mine." -- *(Rick Blaine in Casablanca)*

- "**We shall** go on to the end, **we shall** fight in France, **we shall** fight on the seas and oceans, **we shall** fight with growing confidence and growing strength in the air, **we shall** defend our Island, whatever the cost may be, **we shall** fight on the beaches, **we shall** fight on the landing grounds, **we shall** fight in the fields and in the streets, **we shall** fight in the hills; we shall never surrender."-- *(Winston Churchill, speech to the House of Commons, June 4, 1940)*

- "**Let both sides** explore what problems unite us instead of belaboring those problems which divide us. **Let both sides**, for the first time, formulate serious and precise proposals for the inspection and control of arms, and bring the absolute power to destroy other nations under the absolute control of all nations. "**Let both sides** seek to invoke the wonders of science instead of its terrors. Together let us explore the stars, conquer the deserts, eradicate disease, tap the ocean depths, and encourage the arts and commerce. "**Let both sides** unite to heed, in all corners of the earth, the command of Isaiah--to 'undo the heavy burdens, and to let the oppressed go free.'"-- *(President John Kennedy, Inaugural Address, January 20, 1961)*

- "But **one hundred years later**, the Negro still is not free. **One hundred years later**, the life of the Negro is still sadly crippled by the manacles of segregation and the chains of discrimination. **One hundred years later**, the Negro lives on a lonely island of poverty in the midst of a vast ocean of material prosperity. **One hundred years later**, the Negro is still languishing in the corners of American society and finds himself an exile in his own land. And so we've come here today to dramatize a shameful condition."-- *(Dr. Martin Luther King, Jr., "I Have a Dream," 1963)*

- "It's **the hope** of slaves sitting around a fire singing freedom songs; **the hope** of immigrants setting out for distant shores; **the hope** of a young naval lieutenant bravely patrolling the Mekong Delta; **the hope** of a millworker's son who dares to defy the odds; **the hope** of a skinny kid with a funny name who believes that America has a place for him, too."-- *(Barack Obama, "The*

Audacity of Hope," July 27, 2004)

- **It was** the best of times, **it was** the worst of times, **it was** the age of wisdom, **it was** the age of foolishness, **it was** the epoch of belief, **it was** the epoch of incredulity, **it was** the season of Light, **it was** the season of Darkness, **it was** the spring of hope, **it was** the winter of despair. -- *(A Tale of Two Cities by Charles Dickens)*
- **Segregation** now, **segregation** tomorrow, **segregation** forever... --(George Wallace)
- "Yesterday, the Japanese government also launched an attack against Malaya. **Last night, Japanese forces attacked** Hong Kong. **Last night, Japanese forces attacked** Guam. **Last night, Japanese forces attacked** the Philippine Islands. Last night, **the Japanese attacked** Wake Island. And this morning, **the Japanese attacked** Midway Island." -- *(Franklin Delano Roosevelt, Pearl Harbor Address)*
- "**What we need in the United States is not** division. **What we need in the United States is not** hatred. **What we need in the United States is not** violence and lawlessness; but is love and wisdom and compassion toward one another, and a feeling of justice toward those who still suffer within our country whether they be white or whether they be black."-- *(Robert F. Kennedy, Announcing the death of Martin Luther King)*
- "**We are a people in** a quandary about the present. **We are a people in** search of our future. **We are a people in** search of a national community." -- *(Barbara Jordan, 1976 Democratic Convention Keynote Address)*
- "The Republicans believe that the wagon train will not make it to the frontier unless **some of the** old, **some of the** young, **some of the** weak are left behind by the side of trail."-- *(Mario Cuomo, 1984 Democratic National Convention Address)*
- "To raise a happy, healthy, and hopeful child, **it takes** a family; **it takes** teachers; **it takes** clergy; **it takes** business people; **it takes** community leaders; **it takes** those who protect our health and safety. **It takes** all of us." -- *(Hillary Clinton, 1996 Democratic National Convention Address)*

- "That my heart has been troubled, **that I** have not sought this nomination, **that** I could not seek it in good conscience, **that** I would not seek it in honest self-appraisal, is not to say **that** I value it the less. Rather, it is **that I** revere the office of the Presidency of the United States." -- *(Adlai Stevenson, 1952 DNC Presidential Nomination Acceptance Address)*

Rhetorical Device 8 – Anesis

Anesis is the addition of a phrase, clause or sentence that diminishes the impact of preceding remarks. It is generally placed as the concluding clause or phrase making it as the highlight of the idea.

<u>Examples</u>

- He is the best in this game. His skills, strength and stamina are above most of his competitors. His commitment is deeper than most of his team members. But, **his injury will restrict him to play in this game.**
- He was one of the most admired men of his time, yet he had **one terrible, fatal flaw.**
- This is the best mixer money can buy, although it **does not have a great reputation for reliability.**
- I love you without question. I adore you, above all others. But **I'm not sure I want to go out with you.**
- He was energetic, articulate, popular, and **overconfident**
- "This year's space budget is three times what it was in January 1961, and it is greater than the space budget of the previous eight years combined. That budget now stands at 5 billion, 400 million dollars a year, a staggering sum, **though somewhat less than we pay for cigarettes and cigars every year.**"

CHAPTER NINE

Rhetorical Device 9 – Antanagoge

In Antanagoge a negative point is balanced with a positive point. It is used to create rhetorical impact by perceiving something in a positive way, which is generally acknowledged to be negative, undesirable or difficult.

<u>**Examples**</u>

- "Many are the paines and perils to be passed. But great is the gaine and glorie at the last."
- "When life gives you lemons, make lemonade."
- True, he always forgets my birthday, but he buys me presents all year round.
- He is the worst husband, but he loves me too.
- I lost my business, but I gained experience.
- Tim rarely studies for his examinations, even then people expect him to score high.
- Your words have no value, even then I seems to trust you.

CHAPTER TEN

Rhetorical Device 10 – Antimetabole

Antimetabole is the repetition of words, in successive clauses or phrases, in reverse grammatical order to create emphasis and to deliver a memorable meaning, e.g. A-B, B-A. The whole sentence delivers a notable message which captures the attention of the subject by creating rhetorical impact.

<u>Examples</u>

- When the **going** gets **tough**, the **tough** get **going**.
- Ask not what your **country** can do for **you**; ask what **you** can do for your **country**. *(John F. Kennedy)*
- You can take the **gorilla** out of the **jungle**, but you can't take the **jungle** out of the **gorilla**.

<u>Other Examples</u>

- **Integrity** without **knowledge** is weak and useless, and **knowledge** without **integrity** is dangerous and dreadful. — *(Samuel Johnson, Rasselas)*
- "**Eat** to **live**, not **live** to **eat**."
- "A government that seizes control of the **economy** for the good of the **people**, ends up seizing control of the **people** for the good of the **economy**."-- *(Senator Robert Dole in his acceptance speech for the Republican nomination for president, San Diego, August*

1996)

- "If a **conservative** is a **liberal** who has been mugged, a **liberal** is a **conservative** who has been indicted." -- *(Jeffrey Rosen, The New Yorker)*
- In the U.S., all **crimes are illegalities** but not all **illegalities are crimes.**"
- "The **absence of evidence** is not the **evidence of absence.**" – *(Carl Sagan)*
- "Therefore the treasures of the Gospel are nets with which they formerly were wont to fish for **men of riches.** The treasures of the indulgences are nets with which they now fish for the **riches of men.**" -- *(Luther, Ninety-Five Theses)*
- "I don't throw **darts at balloons.** I throw **balloons at darts.**" – *(Joe Montana on his throwing velocity)*
- "We gotta **play** with **emotion** but not let **emotion play** with us." – *(Coach Chip Kelly, 2011 University of Oregon vs. Arizona State University football game halftime remarks)*
- "We do not **stop playing because we grow old; we grow old because we stop playing.**" – *(Benjamin Franklin)*
- "Those who can't **do -- teach;** and those who can't **teach -- do.**" – *(Delivered by Sarah Jessica Parker - Sex and The City, Episode "Frenemies")*
- "The **richer they get, the tighter they become;** and the **tighter they become, the richer they get.**"
- "Man is not a **creature** of **circumstances. Circumstances** are the **creatures** of men." – *(Benjamin Disraeli)*
- "When **you look into an abyss,** the **abyss also looks into you.**" – *(Frederick Nietzsche)*
- "Hate destroys a man's sense of values and his objectivity. It causes him to describe the **beautiful** as **ugly** and the **ugly** as **beautiful,** and to confuse the **true with the false** and the **false with the true.**" *(Dr. Martin Luther King, Jr.)*
- "I can write **better** than anybody who can write **faster,** and I can write **faster** than anybody who can write **better.**" *(A. J. Liebling)*

- "Good **judgment** comes from **experience** and **experience** comes from bad **judgment**."
- "As far as the laws of mathematics **refer to reality**, they are not **certain**; as far as they are **certain**, they do not **refer to reality**."
- The need for man to overcome **oppression and violence** without resorting to **violence and oppression**." -- *(Martin Luther King, Jr., Nobel Peace Prize Acceptance Address)*
- If there is one message that echoes forth from this conference, let it be that **human rights are women's rights** and **women's rights are human rights** once and for all." -- *(Hillary Rodham Clinton, Women's Rights Are Human Rights)*
- East and West do not **mistrust each other because we are armed; we're armed because we mistrust each other**." -- *(Ronald Reagan, Remarks at the Brandenburg Gage)*
- Let us **preach what we practice** -- let us **practice what we preach**." -- *(Winston Churchill, The Sinews of Peace)*
- Whether we bring **our enemies to justice** or bring **justice to our enemies**, justice will be done." -- *(George W. Bush, 9-20-01 Address to Congress and the Nation)*
- "**The world faces a very different Russia** than it did in 1991. Like all countries, **Russia also faces a very different world**." -- *(William Jefferson Clinton, Address to the Russian Duma)*
- "I, too, was born in the slum. But just because **you're born in the slum** does not mean the **slum is born in you**, and you can rise above it if your mind is made up." -- *(Jesse Jackson, 1984 Democratic National Convention Address)*
- "And so, my fellow Americans, ask not what **your country can do for you**; ask what **you can do for your country**." -- *(John F. Kennedy, Inaugural Address)*
- Each increase of **tension** has produced an increase of **arms**; each increase of **arms** has produced an increase of **tension**. -- *(John F. Kennedy, Limited Nuclear Test Ban Treaty Address to the Nation)*
- **Freedom** requires **religion** just as **religion** requires **freedom**. -- *(Mitt Romney, Faith in America Address, College Station, TX)*

CHAPTER ELEVEN

Rhetorical Device 11 – Antiphrasis

Antiphrasis is used to bring attention to an idea through the use of words in humorous or sarcastic way to present an opposite meaning than the generally accepted implication. It creates the rhetorical impact by making the subject to take efforts for deciphering the true meaning of the statement.

<u>Examples</u>

- Referring to a tall person: "Now there's a midget for you"
- Oh, I am so beautiful! My long nose and pimple so attractive!
- I am but a child of sixty years.
- That is the worst performance I have seen. Oh, look at your face! -- actually I loved it.
- "Yes, I killed him. I killed him for money--and a woman--and I didn't get the money and I didn't get the woman. Pretty, isn't it?" -- *(Fred MacMurray as Walter Neff in Double Indemnity, 1944)*
- "I was awakened by the dulcet tones of Frank, the morning doorman, alternately yelling my name, ringing my doorbell, and pounding on my apartment door." -- *(Dorothy Samuels, Filthy Rich. William Morrow, 2001)*
- "I told you, she's got tracking devices in our fillings! If you two geniuses had ripped them out like I did, we wouldn't have been in this mess!" -- *(Justin Berfield as Reese in "Billboard." Malcolm in the Middle, 2005)*

- "Come here, Tiny," he said to the fat man.
- It was a cool 115 degrees in the shade.
- He is greatest of the great, but he talks cheap.
- He eats too much but his size is extremely small.

CHAPTER TWELVE

Rhetorical Device 12 – Antithesis

The Dictionary meaning of Antithesis is "the state of two things that are directly opposite to each other". It provides the rhetorical contrasting effect in the same sentence, clause or phrase, using the divergent elements but presented as one. It creates rhetorical impact by presenting an interesting idea by balancing the opposite qualities of the subject for deeper insights.

<u>**Examples**</u>

- To err is human; to forgive, divine. – *(Pope)*
- Man proposes, God disposes.
- "Love is an ideal thing, marriage a real thing." *(Goethe)*
- "We must learn to **live together as brothers** or **perish together as fools.**" *(Martin Luther King, Jr.)*
- **Give every man thy ear,** but **few thy voice**
- **Many are called,** but **few are chosen.**
- Money is the root of all evils: poverty is the fruit of all goodness.
- Too black for heaven, and yet too white for hell. – *(By John Dryden)*
- Speech is silver, but Silence is Gold.
- **"Everybody doesn't like something,** but **nobody doesn't like Sara Lee."** -- *(Advertising slogan)*
- **"The world will little note, nor long remember what we say here,** but **it can never forget what they did here."** -- *(Abraham*

Lincoln, The Gettysburg Address, 1863)

- "The **more acute the experience,** the **less articulate its expression.**" -- *(Harold Pinter)*
- "I have a dream that my four little children will one day live in a nation where they will **not be judged by the color of their skin** but **by the content of their character.** I have a dream today!" -- *(Martin Luther King, Jr., I Have a Dream)*
- "We observe today **not a victory of party** but **a celebration of freedom,** symbolizing **an end as well as a beginning,** signifying **renewal as well as change.**" -- *(John F. Kennedy, Inaugural Address)*
- "We find ourselves **rich in goods** but **ragged in spirit, reaching with magnificent precision for the moon** but **falling into raucous discord on earth.** We are **caught in war, wanting peace.** We're **torn by division, wanting unity.**" -- *(Richard M. Nixon, Inaugural Address)*

CHAPTER THIRTEEN

Rhetorical Device 13 – Apophasis

Apophasis is figure of speech in which a subject, topic or idea is specified by mentioning that it will not be stated. This device is often used in political speeches to attack one's opponent by bringing an ironical point about him and simultaneously denying the intention to specify the subject.

<u>Examples</u>

- "I find it interesting that it was back in the 1970s that the swine flu broke out then under another Democrat president, Jimmy Carter. And I'm not blaming this on President Obama. I just think it's an interesting coincidence." -- *(Republican Representative Michele Bachmann, April 28, 2009)*

- "I'm not going to throw mud at my opponent, because he's a fine man. And his wife is a mighty fine woman. Mighty fine. What he sees in that dame he's running around with . . .." -- *(Politician San Fernando Red, portrayed by comedian Red Skelton)*

- "Mary Matlin, the Bush campaign's political director, made the point with ruthless venom at a press briefing in Washington, saying, 'The larger issue is that Clinton is evasive and slick. We have never said to the press that he is a philandering, pot-smoking, draft-dodger. There's nothing nefarious or subliminal going on.'" -- *(Reported in The Guardian, 1992)*

- "I'm not saying I'm responsible for this country's longest run of uninterrupted peace in 35 years! I'm not saying that from the ashes of captivity, never has a phoenix metaphor been more personified! I'm not saying Uncle Sam can kick back on a lawn chair, sipping on an iced tea, because I haven't come across anyone man enough to go toe to toe with me on my best day! It's not about me." -- *(Robert Downey, Jr. as Tony Stark in Iron Man 2, 2010)*

- "I shall ignore the fact that Learning is youth's finest ornament, the strong support of the prime of life, and the consolation of old age. I shall make no point of the fact that, after careers full of achievement and glory, many of the men who have been most honored by their contemporaries and many of the most eminent of the Romans withdrew from the conflict and hurly-burly of ambition to literary studies, as to a harbor and a delightful treat." -- *(John Milton, "Learning Makes Men Happier Than Does Ignorance." Prolusions, 1674)*

- We will not bring up the matter of the budget deficit here, or how programs like the one under consideration have nearly pushed us into bankruptcy, because other reasons clearly enough show . . . .

- Therefore, let no man talk to me of other expedients: of taxing our absentees . . . of curing the expensiveness of pride, vanity, idleness, and gaming of learning to love our country . . . .— *(Jonathan Swift)*

- If you were not my father, I would say you were perverse. – *(Antigone)*

- I will not even mention Houdini's many writings, both on magic and other subjects, nor the tricks he invented, nor his numerous impressive escapes, since I want to concentrate on.

- She's bright, well-read, and personable--to say nothing of her modesty and generosity.

CHAPTER FOURTEEN

Rhetorical Device 14 - Aporia

Aporia is used to create the rhetorical impact by expressing real, pretended or simulated doubt, uncertainty or confusion. In this expression the speaker may present confusion about what to say or where to begin or anything else to appear perplexed or directionless.

<u>Examples</u>

- Maybe I am stupid, or something. Maybe I am not paying attention here. Or maybe you are talking rubbish.
- Now, ladies and gentlemen, would you say that was the worst joke I have told? Or was it the best joke? Funny, that. I can't tell either.
- I am not sure whether to side with those who say that higher taxes reduce inflation or with those who say that higher taxes increase inflation.
- I have never been able to decide whether I really approve of dress codes, because extremism seems to reign both with them and without them.
- "I don't think it's proving anything, Doc. As a matter of fact, I don't even know what it means. It's just one of those things that gets in my head and keeps rolling around in there like a marble." -- *(Peter Falk as Lieutenant Columbo in the episode "Double Exposure," Columbo, 1973)*

- "A virginal air, large blue eyes very soulful and appealing, a dazzling fair skin, a supple and resilient body, a touching voice, teeth of ivory and the loveliest blond hair--there you have a sketch of this charming creature whose naive graces and delicate traits are beyond our power to describe." -- *(Marquis De Sade)*
- "Am I no better than a eunuch or is the proper man--the man with the right to existence--a raging stallion forever neighing after his neighbor's womankind? Or are we meant to act on impulse alone? It is all a darkness." -- *(Ford Maddox Ford, The Good Soldier, 1915)*
- "I gathered my thoughts and tried to appear calm. I was never comfortable dealing with cops, even though their world fascinated me. I always felt that they might suspect something about me. Something bad. Some telling flaw in me.
- "'I'm not sure where to begin. I'm from Denver. I just got in this morning. I'm a reporter and I came across--'" -- *(Michael Connelly, The Poet. Little Brown and Company, 1996)*

CHAPTER FIFTEEN

Rhetorical Device 15 – Aposiopesis

In this figure of speech the speaker leaves the sentence, statement or thought incomplete by suddenly breaking off. The reasons maybe 'the inability or unwillingness to continue or to complete it' or 'intentional for a specific objective'. This can be utilized to create rhetorical impact by leaving the listeners at a point where they would try to understand or visualize the remaining idea or ask for more or remain confused.

<u>Examples</u>

- If they use that section of the desert for bombing practice, the rock hunters will ...
- I've got to make the team or I'll ...
- "Almira Gulch, just because you own half the county doesn't mean that you have the power to run the rest of us. For 23 years I've been dying to tell you what I thought of you! And now--well, being a Christian woman, I can't say it!" -- *(Auntie Em in The Wizard of Oz, 1939)*
- "I will have such revenges on you both, That all the world shall-- I will do things--, What they are yet, I know not; but they shall be, The terrors of the earth!" -- *(William Shakespeare, King Lear)*
- "I won't sleep in the same bed with a woman who thinks I'm lazy! I'm going right downstairs, unfold the couch, unroll the sleeping ba--uh, goodnight." -- *(Homer Simpson in The Simpsons)*

- "Dear Ketel One Drinker--There comes a time in everyone's life when they just want to stop what they're doing and . . ." -- *(Print ad for Ketel One vodka, 2007)*
- "All quiet on Howth now. The distant hills seem. Where we. The rhododendrons. I am a fool perhaps." -- *(James Joyce, Ulysses)*
- "She looked perplexed for a moment, and then said, not fiercely, but still loud enough for the furniture to hear: "'Well, I lay if I get hold of you I'll--', "She did not finish, for by this time she was bending down and punching under the bed with the broom ..." -- *(Aunt Polly in Mark Twain's The Adventures of Tom Sawyer, 1876)*
- "And there's Bernie layin', On the couch, drinkin' a beer, And chewin'--no, not chewin'--poppin'.
- So I said to him, I said, 'Bernie, you pop that, Gum one more time . . .', And he did., So I took the shotgun off the wall, And I fired two warning shots . . ., Into his head." -- *("Cell Block Tango," from Chicago, 2002)*
- "At this juncture I want to get into -- By the way I was told to give you some advice about the media. You don't know how small I feel giving you advice, but I'll be glad to anyway since I've been asked to." -- *(Rush Limbaugh, Address to the incoming House GOP Freshmen)*
- Charlotte Blackwood: "The MiG-28 does have a problem with its inverted flight tanks. It won't do a Negative G push over. The latest intelligence tells us that the most it will do is one negative -- Excuse me, Lieutenant, is there something wrong?" -- *(Delivered by Kelly McGillis from the movie Top Gun)*
- Dr. Petrov: "This is most unnerving, Captain. The reason for having two missile keys is so that no one man may -- ". Captain Ramius: "May what?" -- *(Delivered by Tim Curry and Sean Connery from the movie The Hunt for Red October)*

CHAPTER SIXTEEN

Rhetorical Device 16 – Apostrophe

When a speaker or writer uses an apostrophe for rhetorical impact he tends to detach himself from the rational facts and addresses imaginary or nonexistent thing or person. It is assumed by the speaker or writer that the addressed thing or person is capable of understanding them. Creative people uses apostrophe in various ways in literature and poetry for beautiful representations.

<u>Examples</u>

- "Twinkle, twinkle, little star, How I wonder what you are. Up above the world so high, Like a diamond in the sky." -- *(Jane Taylor, "The Star," 1806)*
- "Blue Moon, you saw me standing alone, Without a dream in my heart, Without a love of my own."-- *(Lorenz Hart, "Blue Moon")*
- "Oh! Stars and clouds and winds, ye are all about to mock me; if ye really pity me, crush sensation and memory; let me become as nought; but if not, depart, depart, and leave me in darkness."-- *(Mary Shelley, Frankenstein, 1818)*
- "Bright star, would I were steadfast as thou art" -- *(John Keats)*
- "Welcome, O life! I go to encounter for the millionth time the reality of experience and to forge in the smithy of my soul the uncreated conscience of my race." -- *(James Joyce, A Portrait of the Artist as a Young Man)*

- "Then come, sweet death, and rid me of this grief." -- *(Queen Isabella in Edward II by Christopher Marlowe)*
- "Ah Bartleby! Ah Humanity!" – *(From 'Bartleby, the Scrivener' by Herman Melville)*
- "O black night, nurse of the golden eyes!" – *(from Euripides' Electra by David Kovacs)*
- Jerusalem, Jerusalem, the city that kills the prophets and stones those sent to her! How often I wanted to gather your children together, just as a hen gathers her brood under her wings, and you would not have it!
- Books who alone are liberal and free, who give to all who ask of you and enfranchise all who serve you faithfully! – *(Richard de Bury)*
- "Roll on thou dark and deep Blue Ocean." – *(from "Childe Harold's Pilgrimage" by Lord Byron)*
- "Oh! Stars and clouds and winds, ye are all about to mock me; if ye really pity me, crush sensation and memory; let me become as nought; but if not, depart, depart, and leave me in darkness."- *(From Frankenstein by Mary Shelly)*

CHAPTER SEVENTEEN

Rhetorical Device 17 – Appositio or Apposition

Appositio is the phrase which provides more details about another word in the same sentence. These extra phrases or clauses can deliver extra information about the noun which can easily be omitted from the sentence without changing its meaning. Its purpose is to provide more information about the word or phrase so as to highlight and emphasize it.

For example, in the phrase "my friend Jack", the name "Jack" is in apposition to "my friend".

<u>**Examples**</u>

- Barry Goldwater, **the junior senator from Arizona**, received the Republican nomination in 1964.
- John and Bob, **both friends of mine**, are starting a band.
- Alexander the Great, **the Macedonian conqueror of Persia**, was one of the most successful military commanders of the ancient world.
- Dean Martin, **a very popular singer**, will be performing at the Sands Hotel
- "I, **Barbara Jordan**, am a keynote speaker."
- "I am elated by the knowledge that for the first time in our history **a woman, Geraldine Ferraro**, will be recommended to share our ticket."

- "**Here, in the great, liberal state of Massachusetts, the cradle of liberty and abolitionism,** a woman was arrested on a minor criminal charge."
- "**John Fitzgerald Kennedy, a great and good President, a friend of all people of goodwill, a believer in the dignity and equality of all human beings, a fighter for justice, an apostle of peace,** has been snatched from our midst by the bullet of an assassin." -- *(Justice Earl Warren, Eulogy for John F. Kennedy)*
- "Miniver Cheevy, **child of scorn**, grew lean while he assailed the seasons."
- "This was not Aunt Dahlia, **my good and kindly aunt**, but my Aunt Agatha, **the one who chews broken bottles and kills rats with her teeth.**" -- *(P.G. Wodehouse)*
- "Gussie, **a glutton for punishment**, stared at himself in the mirror." -- *(P.G. Wodehouse, Right Ho, Jeeves, 1934)*
- **A hot tempered cricket player**, Peter literally tried to crack the wicket keeper's skull.
- **Your sister**, Mary got through her exams with first class.
- Maya, **a bold innovator**, is famous for her artistic painting collections at school.
- The City of Mexico, **a large city**, is recorded to be heavily polluted.
- "The Otis Elevator Company, **the world's oldest and biggest elevator manufacturer**, claims that its products carry the equivalent of the world's population every five days. -- *("Up and Then Down" , Nick Paumgarten, April, 2008)*
- "My father, **a fat, funny man with beautiful eyes and a subversive wit**, is trying to decide which of his eight children he will take with him to the county fair." -- *("Beauty: When the Other Dancer Is The Self, Alice Walker, 1983)*
- "The Koeberg Nuclear Power Station, **Africa's only nuclear power plant**, was inaugurated in 1984 by the apartheid regime and is the major source of electricity for the Western Cape's 4.5 million population." -- *(Joshua Hammer, "Inside Cape Town," April 2008)*

- "Though her cheeks were high-colored and her teeth strong and yellow, she looked like a mechanical woman, **a machine with flashing, glassy circles for eyes.**" -- *(Kate Simon, 'Bronx Primitive', 1982)*

- The village of Holcomb stands on the high wheat plains of western Kansas, **a lonesome area that other Kansans call 'out there'.** -- *(Truman Capote, 'In Cold Blood)*

- "I have had the great honor to have played with these great veteran ballplayers on my left--Murderers Row, **our championship team of 1927.** I have had the further honor of living with and playing with these men on my right--the Bronx Bombers, **the Yankees of today.**" -- *(The Pride of the Yankees, Gary Cooper as Lou Gehrig, 1942)*

- "The Spectator. **Champagne for the brain.**" -- *(Ad slogan for The Spectator magazine)*

- "Xerox. **The Document Company.**" -- *(Slogan of Xerox Corporation)*

- "Dr. John Harvey Kellogg, **inventor of the cornflake and peanut butter, not to mention caramel-cereal coffee, Bromose, Nuttolene, and some seventy-five other gastronomically correct foods,** paused to level his gaze on the heavyset women in front of him." -- *(T. Coraghassen Boyle, The Road to Wellville. Viking, 1993)*

- "The sky was sunless and grey, there was snow in the air, **buoyant motes, play things that seethed and floated like the toy flakes inside a crystal.**" -- *(Truman Capote, "The Muses Are Heard")*

- "Nothing contributes so much to tranquilize the mind as a steady purpose--**a point on which the soul may fix its intellectual eye.**" -- *(Mary Wollstonecraft Shelley, letter I in Frankenstein, 1818)*

CHAPTER EIGHTEEN

Rhetorical Device 18 – Assonance

Assonance is the use of words which are placed closed to one another that repeat the same vowel sound but starts with different consonant sounds. Put simply, assonance is the repetition of a pattern of similar sounds within a sentence so as to create a rhythm and to make it memorable. It is used in poetry to create different effects. For example:

- Do **you** like **blue**? (Please note the highlighted words)
- Take the **gun** and have **fun**.
- **Play** with the **clay** to make the dolls.
- **Ba**ke the **ca**ke and eat quickly.
- **He** received **three**emails today.

Examples

- "If I bleat when I speak it's because I just got . . . fleeced." -- *(Al Swearengen in Deadwood, 2004)*
- "It beats . . . as it sweeps . . . as it cleans!" -- *(Advertising slogan for Hoover vacuum cleaners, 1950s)*
- "Those images that yet, Fresh images beget, That dolphin-torn, that gong-tormented sea." -- *(W.B. Yeats, "Byzantium")*
- "The spider skins lie on their sides, translucent and ragged, their legs drying in knots." -- *(Annie Dillard, Holy the Firm, 1977)*

- "The setting sun was licking the hard bright machine like some great invisible beast on its knees." -- *(John Hawkes, Death, Sleep, and the Traveler, 1974)*
- "I must confess that in my quest I felt depressed and restless." -- *(Thin Lizzy, "With Love")*
- "In the over-mastering loneliness of that moment, his whole life seemed to him nothing but vanity." -- *(Robert Penn Warren, Night Rider, 1939)*
- "A lanky, six-foot, pale boy with an active Adam's apple, ogling Lo and her orange-brown bare midriff, which I kissed five minutes later, Jack." -- *(Vladimir Nabokov, Lolita, 1955)*
- "Strips of tinfoil winking like people" -- *(Sylvia Plath, "The Bee Meeting")*
- "Betty bought butter but the butter was bitter, so Betty bought better butter to make the bitter butter better."
- As I was going to St. Ives, I met a man with seven wives, Every wife had seven sacks, every sack had seven cats, Every cat had seven kittens: kittens, cats, sacks and wives, How many were going to St. Ives?" -- *(Delivered by Jeremy Irons, from the movie Die Hard with a Vengeance as taken from the riddle poem "As I was going to St. Ives")*
- "The gloves didn't fit. If it doesn't fit, you must acquit." -- *(Johnny Cochran, Closing Arguments from the O.J. Simpson Trial)*
- "When Jesus told his disciples to pray for the kingdom, this was no pie in the sky by and by when you die kind of prayer." -- *(Tony Campolo)*
- "In the brief span of thirty-odd years, the world has seen an inventors dream, first materialized by the Wright brothers at Kitty Hawk, become an everyday actuality." – *(Amelia Earhart)*
- "Our flag is red, white, and blue -- but our nation is rainbow. Red, yellow, brown, black, and white, we're all precious in God's sight." -- *(Jesse Jackson, 1984 Democratic National Convention Address)*
- "I feel the need, the need for speed." -- *(Delivered by Tom Cruise and Anthony Edwards from the movie Top Gun)*

CHAPTER NINETEEN

Rhetorical Device 19 - Asyndeton

Asyndeton is the practice in communication whereby the speaker or author intentionally leaves the generally used conjunctions like and, or, but, for, nor, so, yet, from the sentence, clause or phrase to create a dramatic effect on the listener or reader. It is to be noted that the grammatical accuracy of the phrase is maintained while using this rhetorical device. This creates a compact version of the entire phrase which can put instant rhetorical impact on the listener.

<u>Examples</u>

- On his return he received medals, **honors, treasures, titles, fame**.
- They spent the day wondering, **searching, thinking, understanding**.
- He was **a winner, a hero**.
- "He was a bag of bones, **a floppy doll, a broken stick, a maniac**." -- *(Jack Kerouac, On the Road, 1957)*
- "It is a northern country; **they have cold weather, they have cold hearts**.
- "Cold; **tempest; wild** beasts in the forest. It is a hard life. Their houses are built of logs, dark and smoky within. There will be a crude icon of the virgin behind a guttering candle, **the leg of a pig hung up to cure, a string of drying mushrooms**. A bed,

a stool, a table. Harsh, **brief, poor** lives." -- *(Angela Carter, "The Werewolf." The Bloody Chamber and Other Stories, 1979)*

- "I have found the warm caves in the woods, filled them with skillets, **carvings, shelves,closets, silks, innumerable goods**" -- *(Anne Sexton, "Her Kind")*

- "Anyway, like I was saying, shrimp is the fruit of the sea. You can barbecue it, **boil it, broil it, bake it, saute it.** Dey's uh, shrimp-kabobs, **shrimp creole, shrimp gumbo.** Pan fried, **deep fried, stir-fried.** There's pineapple shrimp, **lemon shrimp, coconut shrimp, pepper shrimp, shrimp soup, shrimp stew, shrimp salad, shrimp and potatoes, shrimp burger, shrimp sandwich.** That--that's about it." -- *(Bubba in Forrest Gump, 1994)*

- "In some ways, he was this town at its best--strong, **hard-driving, working feverishly, pushing, building, driven** by ambitions so big they seemed Texas-boastful." -- *(Mike Royko, "A Tribute")*

- He received applause, **prizes, money, fame.**

- He provided her education, **allowance, dignity.**

- I could have gone to **war, I** didn't.

- He tried to betray you, **to cheat you, to deceive you.**

- Smile, **talk, bye-bye.**

- We met, **we got engaged, we married.**

- She is addicted to chocolates, **cakes, cookies.**

- "I came, **I saw, I conquered**". -- *(Translated from the Latin saying 'Veni, Vidi, Vici' these are words by Julius Caesar describing one of his greatest victories)*

- "...and that government of the people, **by the people, for the people** shall not perish from the earth." -- *(Quoted by Abraham Lincoln at the Gettysburg Address)*

- "...that we shall pay any price, **bear any burden, meet any hardship, support any friend, oppose any foe** to assure the survival and the success of liberty." -- *(From John F. Kennedys Inaugural Address of 1961)*

- "We must... hold them, **as we hold the rest of mankind, Enemies in War, in Peace Friends.**" -- *(The US Declaration of*

Independence referring to the British)

- "We shall go on to the end, **we shall fight in France, we shall fight on the seas and oceans, we shall fight with growing confidence and growing strength in the air, we shall defend our Island, whatever the cost may be, we shall fight on the beaches, we shall fight on the landing grounds, we shall fight in the fields and in the streets, we shall fight in the hills; we shall never surrender. . . "** -- *(From Winston Churchill's address popularly known as 'We shall fight on the beaches<' in 1940)*
- **He comes, he sleeps, he goes**
- "Duty, **Honor, Country**: Those three hallowed words reverently dictate what you ought to be, **what you can be, what you will be.** They are your rallying points: to build courage when courage seems to fail; **to regain faith when there seems to be little cause for faith; to create hope when hope becomes forlorn."** -- *(General Douglas MacArthur, Thayer Award Acceptance Address)*
- "We use words like honor, **code, loyalty.** We use these words as the backbone of a life spent defending something. You use them as a punch line." -- *(Delivered by Jack Nicholson from the movie A Few Good Men)*

CHAPTER TWENTY

Rhetorical Device 20 – Catachresis

Catachresis is the unusual, outlandish or weird comparison or association made between two completely different things, which are generally not connected in any way in normal language or is at odds with conventional usage to create a rhetorical impact in speech or writing.

<u>Examples</u>

- Her **laughing feet** fell overboard with amazement.
- He looked at the price and his **pockets ran dry**.
- She grabbed the bull by the **horns of the dilemma**.
- He was as **happy as a corpse**.
- **A table's leg**
- "**Darkness visible**" – (John Milton, Paradise Lost)
- "To take arms against a **sea of troubles**..." – (Shakespeare, Hamlet)
- "The runner literally **flew down the track**."
- "Red trains cough Jewish underwear for keeps! Expanding smells of silence. Gravy snot whistling like sea birds." -- (*Amiri Baraka, The Dutchman*)
- "Honey, you are a regular **nuclear meltdown**. You'd better cool off." -- (*Delivered by Susan Sarandon from the movie Bull Durham*)
- "The President's decision yesterday, to set into motion the development of the hydrogen bomb, has placed us on a **knife**

edge of history." -- *(Henry M. Jackson)*
- "I'm the producer of this show. If I didn't step up, you're nowhere. I put this thing together on a **spit and polish**." -- *(Delivered by Dustin Hoffman from the movie Wag the Dog)*
- "There she stood on stage for all to see, showing off like the **greedy songbird** she was." -- *(Delivered by F. Murray Abraham from the movie Amadeus)*
- "Now the **jet black shadow of our want** and misery came upon us step by step with certain precision, day after day, month after month, and year after year." -- *(Huey P. Long, Saint Vitus Dance Government)*
- "C'mon rook. Show us that million dollar arm 'cause I gotta, oh, I gotta good idea about that **five cent head of yours**." -- *(Delivered by Kevin Costner from the movie Bull Durham)*

CHAPTER TWENTY-ONE

Rhetorical Device 21 – Chiasmus

Chiasmus creates the rhetorical impact through artistic effect with the placement of words. It is like inverted parallelism in which two or more clauses are balanced against each other by reversal of the words, grammatical constructions, or concepts, in similar or altered form. For example – Never let a **fool kiss** you or a **kiss fool** you.

For Example

- A **hard** man is **good** to find. – *(Mae West)* (Reversing, a **good** man is **hard** to find).
- A **statesman** is a **politician** who places himself at the **service** of the **nation**. (Or, a **politician** is a **statesman** who places the **nation** at his **service**).
- I'd rather have a **bottle** in **front** of me than a **front**al lobotomy. – *(Winston Churchill)*
- A magician pulls rabbits out of hats. (Instead of, an experimental psychologist pulls **habits** out of **rats**).
- A lawyer starts life giving **$500** worth of law for **$5** and ends giving **$5** worth for **$500**.
- Lust is what makes you keep wanting to do it, Even when you have no desire to be with each other. Love is what makes you keep wanting to be with each other, Even when you have no desire to do it. – *(Judith Viorst)*

<u>Other Examples</u>

- She would rather **fool** with a **bee** than **be** with a **fool**. – *(John Kendrick Bangs)*
- This isn't a bar for **writers with a drinking problem**; it's for **drinkers with a writing problem**. – *(Judy Joice)*
- The value of marriage is not that **adults produce children**, but that **children produce adults**. – *(Peter de Vries)*
- Do **I love you** because **you're beautiful?**
  Or are **you beautiful** because **I love you?** – *(Oscar Hammerstein)*
- They don't **care about how much you know** until they **know how much you care** – *(Jim Calhoun)*
- I find Paul app**eal**ing
  and Peale app**all**ing. – *(Adlai Stevenson)*
- There are **trivial truths** and **great truths**. The opposite of a **trivial truth** is plainly false. The opposite of a **great truth** is also true. – *(Niels Bohr)*
- The art of progress is to **preserve order amid change**, and to **preserve change amid order**. -- *(Alfred North Whitehead)*
- Our very **hopes** belied our **fears**, our **fears** our **hopes** belied; We thought her **dying** when she **slept**, and **sleeping** when she **died**. – *(Thomas Hood)*
- I'd rather be **looked** than over**looked**. – *(Mae West)*
- Some have an idea that the reason we in this country **discard things so readily** is because **we have so much**. The facts are exactly opposite - the reason **we have so much** is simply because **we discard things so readily**. – *(Alfred P. Solan)*
- One should **eat to live**, not **live to eat**. – *(Cicero)*
- In the **70's** I threw in the **90's**;
  In the **90's** I throw in the **70's**. – *(Frank Tanana)*
- Infantile love follows the principle: "**I love** because **I am loved**." Mature love follows the principle: "**I am loved** because **I love**." Immature love says: "**I love you** because **I need you**." Mature love says: "**I need you** because **I love you**." – *(Erich Fromm)*

- **"Nice to see you, to see you, nice!"** -- *(Catchphrase of British TV entertainer Bruce Forsyth)*
- "You forget what you want to remember, and you remember what you want to forget." -- *(Cormac McCarthy, The Road, 2006)*

- "In the end, the true test is not the speeches a president delivers; it's whether the president delivers on the speeches." -- *(Hillary Clinton, March 2008)*
- "I had a teacher I liked who used to say good fiction's job was to comfort the disturbed and disturb the comfortable." -- *(David Foster Wallace)*
- "I flee who chases me, and chase who flees me." -- *(Ovid)*
- "Fair is foul, and foul is fair." -- *(William Shakespeare, Macbeth)*
- "Your manuscript is both good and original; but the part that is good is not original, and the part that is original is not good." -- *(Samuel Johnson)*
- "If black men have no rights in the eyes of the white men, of course the whites can have none in the eyes of the blacks." -- *(Frederick Douglass, "An Appeal to Congress for Impartial Suffrage")*
- "The art of progress is to preserve order amid change and to preserve change amid order." -- *(Alfred North Whitehead)*
- "People the world over have always been more impressed by the power of our example than by the example of our power." -- *(President Bill Clinton, August 2008)*
- "You can take it out of the country, but you can't take the country out of it." -- *(Slogan for Salem cigarettes)*
- "Friendly Americans win American friends." -- *(United States Travel Service, 1963)*
- "Never let a fool kiss you--or a kiss fool you." -- *(Joey Adams, quoted by Mardy Grothe in Never Let a Fool Kiss You or a Kiss Fool You. Viking, 1999)*
- "My job is not to represent Washington to you, but to represent you to Washington." -- *(Barack Obama)*

- "I am stuck on Band-Aid, and Band-Aid's stuck on me." -- *(Advertising jingle for Band-Aid bandages)*
- "Let us never negotiate out of fear, but let us never fear to negotiate." -- *(President John Kennedy, Inaugural Address, January 20, 1961)*

CHAPTER TWENTY-TWO

Rhetorical Device 22 – Climax

Climax is a commonly used figure of speech to create rhetorical impact by placing words, phrases or sentences in the order of increasing importance. This means that the words with lower significance would be placed before the words and phrases with higher significance, often in parallel structure, thereby forcefully delivering the message.

<u>Examples</u>

- "There are those who are asking the devotees of civil rights, 'When will you be satisfied?' We can never be satisfied as long as the Negro is the victim of the unspeakable horrors of police brutality. We can never be satisfied as long as our bodies, heavy with the fatigue of travel, cannot gain lodging in the motels of the highways and the hotels of the cities. We cannot be satisfied as long as the Negro's basic mobility is from a smaller ghetto to a larger one. We can never be satisfied as long as our children are stripped of their self-hood and robbed of their dignity by a sign stating 'For Whites Only.' We cannot be satisfied as long as a Negro in Mississippi cannot vote and a Negro in New York believes he has nothing for which to vote. No, no, we are not satisfied, and we will not be satisfied until justice rolls down like waters, and righteousness like a mighty stream." -- *(Martin Luther King, Jr., "I Have a Dream." August 28, 1963)*

- "When we send our young men and women into harm's way, we have a solemn obligation not to fudge the numbers or shade the truth about why they're going, to care for their families while they're gone, to tend to the soldiers upon their return, and to never ever go to war without enough troops to win the war, secure the peace, and earn the respect of the world." -- *(Barack Obama, "The Audacity of Hope," 2004 Democratic National Convention Keynote Address)*

- It is absolutely not right to arrest or detain an innocent man. It is a bigger crime to whip him for a crime he had nothing to do with. All of this is tolerable, but to sentence him to his death when he has wronged not a soul is something that cannot be excused. Such is the state of justice, an innocent man paying ever so dearly for the crime of another.

- "Out of its vivid disorder comes order; from its rank smell rises the good aroma of courage and daring; out of its preliminary shabbiness comes the final splendor. And buried in the familiar boasts of its advance agents lies the modesty of most of its people." -- *(E. B. White, "The Ring of Time")*

- "It may, perhaps, be fairly questioned, whether any other portion of the population of the earth could have endured the privations, sufferings and horrors of slavery, without having become more degraded in the scale of humanity than the slaves of African descent. Nothing has been left undone to cripple their intellects, darken their minds, debase their moral stature, obliterate all traces of their relationship to mankind; and yet how wonderfully they have sustained the mighty load of a most frightful bondage, under which they have been groaning for centuries!" -- *(Frederick Douglass, Narrative of the Life of Frederick Douglass, An American Slave, 1845)*

- My brother need not be idealized, or enlarged in death beyond what he was in life; to be remembered simply as a good and decent man, who saw wrong and tried to right it, saw suffering and tried to heal it, saw war and tried to stop it. Those of us who loved him and who take him to his rest today, pray that what he was to us and what he wished for others will someday come to pass for all the world. -- *(Edward M. Kennedy, Tribute to Senator Robert F. Kennedy, June 8, 1968)*

- "This is the Court of Chancery; which has its decaying houses and its blighted lands in every shire; which has its worn-out lunatic in every madhouse, and its dead in every churchyard; which has its ruined suitor, with his slipshod heels and threadbare dress, borrowing and begging through the round of every man's acquaintance; which gives to monied might, the means abundantly of wearying out the right; which so exhausts finances, patience, courage, hope; so overthrows the brain and breaks the heart; that there is not an honourable man among its practitioners who would not give--who does not often give--the warning, 'Suffer any wrong that can be done you, rather than come here!'" -- *(Charles Dickens, Bleak House, 1852)*
- "All that most maddens and torments; all that stirs up the lees of things; all truth with malice in it; all that cracks the sinews and cakes the brain; all the subtle demonisms of life and thought; all evil, to crazy Ahab, were visibly personified and made practically assailable in Moby Dick." – *(An extract from 'Moby Dick')*
- Let a man acknowledge his obligations to himself, his family, his country, and his God.
- And now abideth faith, hope, charity, these three; but the greatest of these is charity.
- When you step out into the jungle, there are three things that you need to be aware of, the time of day, your whereabouts and wild animals.
- He is uncomplicated, upright, strict, austere and inspirational.
- What a piece of work this is! How holy in reason, how inestimable in faculties! In action, how much like an angel!
- As the bowler walked up to the batsman, he stared him in the eye and challenged him to hit him out of the park. The batsman accepted the challenge. With excitement in his stride, the bowler then rushed in to hurl the ball at the batsman. The hawkeyed

batter was more than prepared. With a quick and sudden twist of his bat, the ball was sent soaring to the stands.

- On her way to work, she met with an accident. This was how it all unfolded. As she began to cross a very street close to where she worked, she was knocked down by a speeding motorist, post the fall, a bus went over her limbs, just missing her abdomen. She managed to survive the mishap, retaining just about an inch of her life.
- "And from the crew of Apollo 8, we close with good night, good luck,a merry Christmas, and God bless all of you, all of you on the good earth." -- *(Frank Borman, Astronaut)*
- "In the beginning was the Word, and the Word was with God, andthe Word was God."
- "Oh, America didn't need repeal, she needed repentance; she didn't need rum, she needed righteousness; we don't need jags, we need Jesus; we don't need more grog, we need more of God." -- *(Billy Sunday, Booze)*

CHAPTER TWENTY-THREE

Rhetorical Device 23 – Conduplicatio

Conduplicatio is the repetition of a word in a sentence or adjacent phrases or clauses, without any particular placement of words, to provide rhetorical impact in the delivery. This sometimes is used to deliver a specific meaning.

<u>Examples</u>

- **War** it is that you are bringing into Attica, Aeschines, an Amphictyonic **war**. -- *(Demosthenes, De corona 143)*
- If this is the first time **duty** has moved him to act against his desires, he is a very weak man indeed. **Duty** should be cultivated and obeyed in spite of its frequent conflict with selfish wishes.
- The strength of the **passions** will never be accepted as an excuse for complying with them; the **passions** were designed for subjection, and if a man suffers them to get the upper hand, he then betrays the liberty of his own soul. – *(Alexander Pope)*
- She fed the goldfish every day with the new pellets brought from Japan. Gradually the goldfish began to turn a brighter orange than before.
- "And now, I stand before you, Mr. President -- Commander-in-Chief of the army that freed me, and tens of thousands of others -- and I am filled with a profound and abiding **gratitude** to the American people. **Gratitude** is a word that I cherish. **Gratitude** is what defines the humanity of the human being." --

(Elie Wiesel, The Perils of Indifference)

- "So I ask you tonight to return home, to say a **prayer** for the family of Martin Luther King -- yeah, it's true -- but more importantly to say a **prayer** for our own country, which all of us love -- a **prayer** for understanding and that compassion of which I spoke. We can do well in this country." -- *(Robert F. Kennedy, Impromptu remarks on the assassination of Martin Luther King, Jr.)*
- "This afternoon, in this room, I testified before the Office of Independent Council and the Grand Jury. I answered their **questions** truthfully, including **questions** about my private life -- **questions** no American citizen would ever want to answer." -- *(William Jefferson Clinton)*
- "Drugs don't just **destroy** their victims; they **destroy** entire families, schools, and communities." -- *(Elizabeth Dole, 1999 San Diego Stump Speech)*
- "I could list the **problems** which cause people to feel cynical, **problems** which include lack of integrity in government, the feeling that the individual no longer counts....'" -- *(Barbara Jordan, 1976 Democratic National Convention Address)*
- "There is no question but that this nation cannot stand still, because we are in a deadly **competition**, a **competition** not only with the men in the Kremlin, but the men in Peking. We're ahead in this **competition**, as Senator Kennedy, I think, has implied. But when you're in a race, the only way to stay ahead is to move ahead." -- *(Richard M. Nixon, Opening Statement, First Debate with John F. Kennedy)*

CHAPTER TWENTY-FOUR

Rhetorical Device 24 – Diacope

Diacope is used to express deep feelings by repeating a word or phrase with one or more intervening words. It is used to create emphasis on an idea by adding similar word or set of words, for repetition, to a sentence or phrase.

<u>Examples</u>

- "And **we read**, incredible as it seems, **we read** of survivors struggling in the water...." -- *(Peter Marshall on the Titanic tragedy)*
- "**Confidence is high** -- I repeat -- **confidence is high**." -- *(From the movie War Games)*
- "The people **everywhere**, not just here in Britain, **everywhere** -- they kept faith with Princess Diana." -- *(Tony Blair)*
- "**Patience**, Iago, **patience**." -- *(Delivered by Jonathan Freeman from the movie Aladdin)*
- **Fire**, hot **fire**, burned across the town.
- **It will be done**. By hook or by crook, **it will be done**.
- '**Why?**' he asked, '**Why?**' And well he might.
- "Scott Farkus staring out at us with his **yellow eyes**. He had **yellow eyes**! So help me, God! **Yellow eyes**!" -- *(Ralphie Parker, A Christmas Story, 1983)*
- "And now, my beauties, something **with poison in it**, I think. **With poison in it**, but attractive to the eye and soothing to the

smell." -- *(The Wicked Witch of the West, The Wizard of Oz, 1939)*

- "In **times like these**, it helps to recall that there have always been **times like these**." -- *(Paul Harvey)*
- "They **will laugh**, indeed they **will laugh**, at his parchment and his wax." -- *(Edmund Burke, "A Letter to a Noble Lord," 1796)*
- "I'm gonna cut out now with this **unusual** song I'm dedicating to an **unusual** person who makes me feel kind of **unusual**." -- *(Christian Slater as Mark Hunter in Pump Up the Volume, 1990)*
- "I knew it. Born **in a hotel room**—and goddamn it—died **in a hotel room**." -- *(Last words of playwright Eugene O'Neill)*
- "It is the tragedy of the world that no one **knows** what he doesn't **know**; and the less a man **knows**, the more sure he is that he **knows** everything." -- *(Joyce Cary, Art & Reality, 1958)*
- "It is explained that all relationships require a little **give** and take. This is untrue. Any partnership demands that we **give** and **give** and **give** and at the last, as we flop into our graves exhausted, we are told that we didn't **give** enough." -- *(Quentin Crisp, Manners From Heaven, 1984)*
- "All happy families are alike, but an **unhappy** family is **unhappy** after its own fashion." -- *(Leo Tolstoy, Anna Karenina, 1877)*
- "I am **neat**, scrupulously **neat**, in regard to the things I care about; but a **book**, as a **book**, is not one of those things." -- *(Max Beerbohm, "Whistler's Writing." The Pall Mall Magazine, 1904)*
- "**Put out the light**, and then **put out the light**." -- *(Othello in William Shakespeare's Othello, the Moor of Venice, Act Five, scene 2)*
- "And now, my beauties, something **with poison in it**, I think. **With poison in it**, but attractive to the eye and soothing to the smell." -- *(The Wicked Witch of the West, The Wizard of Oz, 1939)*
- "**They will laugh**, indeed **they will laugh**, at his parchment and his wax." -- *(Edmund Burke, "A Letter to a Noble Lord," 1796)*
- "I can picture in my mind **a world without** war, **a world without** hate. And I can picture us attacking that world, because they'd

never expect it." -- *(Jack Handey, Deep Thoughts)*

- "I'm gonna cut out now with this **unusual** song I'm dedicating to an **unusual** person who makes me feel kind of **unusual**." -- *(Christian Slater as Mark Hunter in Pump Up the Volume, 1990)*
- "You're not **fullyclean** until you're Zest **fullyclean**." -- *(Advertising slogan for Zest soap)*
- "Blair sounded like a man who had spent the morning riffling through handbooks of classical rhetoric: 'This indulgence has to stop. Because it is **dangerous**. It is **dangerous** if such regimes disbelieve us. **Dangerous** if they think they can use weakness, our hesitation, even the natural urges of our democracy towards peace, against us. **Dangerous** because one day they will mistake our innate revulsion against war for permanent incapacity.'" -- *(Anthony Lane, "The Prime Minister." The New Yorker, March 31, 2003)*
- "The people **everywhere**, not just here in Britain, **everywhere** -- they kept faith with Princess Diana." -- *(Tony Blair)*
- "And **we read**, incredible as it seems, **we read** of survivors struggling in the water...." -- *(Peter Marshall on the Titanic tragedy)*
- "**Confidence is high** -- I repeat -- **confidence is high**." -- *(From the movie War Games)*

CHAPTER TWENTY-FIVE

Rhetorical Device 25 - Dirimens Copulatio

Dirimens Copulatio is the specification of a fact or an idea which is in direct opposition to the statement presented before to prevent the argument from being unqualified or one-sided and to create a balance in the statement.

<u>Examples</u>

- This car is extremely sturdy and durable. It's low maintenance; things never go wrong with it. Of course, if you abuse it, it will break.
- . . . But we preach Christ crucified, to Jews a stumbling block, and to Gentiles foolishness, but to those who are called, both Jews and Greeks, Christ the power of God and the wisdom of God.

CHAPTER TWENTY-SIX

Rhetorical Device 26 - Distinctio

Distinctio is useful in creating rhetorical impact by referring to the multiple meanings of a word or other elaboration in the sentence to clarify, highlight or enquire about the particular meaning intended and to avoid any ambiguity or confusion.

<u>Examples</u>

- When I say **hot**, I do not mean she was **warm** -- I mean she was very **sexy**!
- Now when you say '**rough**', do you mean **difficult** or do you mean **harsh**, because both make sense, although I would have thought the latter most appropriate.
- Now becoming invisible is **impossible**. And by impossible I mean **beyond possibility** within our current technologies.
- "It depends upon what the meaning of the word '**is**' is. If '**is**' means '**is and never has been**,' that's one thing. If it means '**there is none**,' that was a completely true statement." -- *(President Bill Clinton, Grand Jury testimony, 1998)*
- "[I]t would be a long while before I would come to understand the particular moral of the story.

"It would be a long while because, quite simply, I was in love with New York. I do not mean 'love' in any colloquial way, I mean that I was in love with the city, the way you love the first person who ever touches you and never love anyone quite that same way again." -- *(Joan Didion, "Goodbye to All That." Slouching Towards Bethlehem, 1968)*

- "A significant proportion of the detainees held at Guantanamo were picked up far from anything remotely resembling a battlefield. Arrested in cities all over the world, they could only be deemed combatants if one accepts the Bush Administration's claim of a literal 'war on terrorism.' . . . A review of these cases shows that the arresting officers are police, not soldiers, and that the places of arrest include private homes, airports and police stations--not battlefields." -- *(Joanne Mariner, "It All Depends on What You Mean by Battlefield." FindLaw, July 18, 2006)*
- "It was the best of times, it was the -- I say -- worst of times – and by worse I'm talkin' as bad -- I say -- as bad as my aunt Jenny's corn puddin'. That stuff will sink you like a stone." -- *(Delivered by Foghorn Leghorn for GEICO)*
- "We must address ourselves to the fact that if we dare end discrimination against women, **which means if we dare finally take women seriously as people....**" -- *(Betty Friedan, Dare We Not Discriminate?)*
- "Now, first I should define my terms: **'man' and 'God.' By man, of course, I mean society -- social man....**" -- *(Timothy Leary, LSD: Methods of Control)*
- "The great, large achievement of liberalism in the 20th century is the welfare State. And that achievement, today, makes additional liberalism virtually impossible. **By 'additional liberalism' I mean more of the same -- energetic, high-spending, and high tax, redistributionist egalitarian government.**" -- *(George F. Will, John M. Ashbrook Memorial Dinner Address)*
- "Solid security arrangements on the ground are necessary not only to protect the peace; they're necessary to protect Israel in case the peace unravels, because in our unstable region, **no one can guarantee that our peace partners today will be there tomorrow.** And my friends, when I say tomorrow, I don't mean

some distant time in the future; I mean tomorrow." -- *(Benjamin Netanyahu, 2011 Address to Congress)*

- "'Demoralization.' I distinguished in that book **two senses of demoralization: the familiar one of the loss of morale, of contentment, and good spirit -- and the more serious one of the loss of morality, of moral bearings and convictions."** -- *(Gertrude Himmelfarb, John M. Ashbrook Memorial Dinner Address)*

- "I've been in football all my life, really, and I want to say this -- that it's a great game, and it's a **Spartan type of game. I mean by that it takes Spartan qualities in order to be a part of it, to play it. And I speak of the Spartan qualities of sacrifice and self-denial rather than that other Spartan quality of leaving the weak to die."** -- *(Vince Lombardi)*

CHAPTER TWENTY-SEVEN

Rhetorical Device 27 – Enthymeme

Enthymeme is like Syllogism (three part deductive argument), which is informally stated as the part of the argument is missing and is left implied. It has an unspecified assumption which must be true for the premises to lead to the conclusion.

All syllogisms are similar in that they contain at least three statements -- two premises followed by a conclusion.

Example 1:

- All humans are mortal. (major premise)
- Tim is human. (minor premise)
- Tim is mortal. (conclusion)

Example 2:

- Those who study rhetoric speak eloquently. (major premise)
- Susan studies rhetoric. (minor premise)
- Susan speaks eloquently. (conclusion)

Example 3:

"We cannot trust this man, for he has perjured himself in the past."

In this enthymeme, the major premise of the complete syllogism is missing:

- Those who perjure themselves cannot be trusted. (Major premise - omitted)
- This man has perjured himself in the past. (Minor premise - stated)
- This man is not to be trusted. (Conclusion - stated)

Other Examples

- If to be foolish is evil, then it is virtuous to be wise.
- 'He must be a socialist because he favors a graduated income-tax.

- "But Brutus says he was ambitious; And Brutus is an honorable man." – (*Mark Antony from Shakespeare's 'Julius Caesar'*)
- He is an American citizen, so he is entitled to due process. (The hidden premise is: All American citizens are entitled to due process.)
- She could not have committed this horrible crime; I have known her since she was a child.
- A political system can be just only when those who make its laws keep well informed about the subject and effect of those laws. This is why our system is in danger of growing unjust.
- No minority will be a person who will get this job. I am a minority. Therefore, I am not a person who will get this job.
- "Now, I don't know or have never met my candidate; and for that reason I am more apt to say something good of him than anyone else." – (*Will Rogers*)
- Dependent creatures should be humble. We are dependent creatures. Therefore, we should be humble.
- Bad boys should get spankings. You have been bad. Therefore, you should get spankings.
- Nothing Relieves Pain Faster than Bayer Aspirin. I have pain. I will take Bayer Aspirin.
- "There is no law against composing music when one has no ideas whatsoever. The music of Wagner, therefore, is perfectly legal."

– *(Mark Twain)*

- "The gloves didn't fit. If it doesn't fit, you must acquit." -- *(Johnny Cochran, Closing arguments of the O.J. Simpson trial)*
- If the gloves didn't fit, you must acquit. (Major premise). The gloves didn't fit. (Minor premise). You must acquit. (Conclusion)
- "Now, I don't know or have never met my candidate; and for that reason I am more apt to say something good of him than anyone else." -- *(Will Rogers)*
- I have a goal to do. Carrying out this action is a means to realize the goal. Therefore, I ought to carry out this action.
- The gun has the defendant's fingerprints on the trigger. He is clearly guilty! -- *(Edward P.J. Corbett and Robert J. Connors, Classical Rhetoric for the Modern Student, 4th ed. Oxford Univ. Press, 1999)*
- "Senator, I served with Jack Kennedy. I knew Jack Kennedy. Jack Kennedy was a friend of mine. Senator, you're no Jack Kennedy." – *(Lloyd Bentsen to Dan Quayle, 1988. The hidden premises might be: Jack Kennedy was a great man, and you are not a great man.).* Those who don't know or have never met their candidates are more apt to speak well of them. (Major premise). I don't know or have never met my candidate. (Minor premise). I am more apt to say something good of him. (Conclusion)
- "Ladies and gentlemen, I will not divide the Democratic Party. Therefore, tomorrow morning I will write to the Chairman of the Democratic Party withdrawing my candidacy." -- *(Thomas F. Eagleton).* Those who will not divide the Democratic Party must withdraw their candidacy. (Major premise). I will not divide the Democratic Party. (Minor premise). I will withdraw my candidacy. (Conclusion)
- "I wanted to serve as President because I love this country and because I love the people of this Nation." -- *(Jimmy Carter, 1980 Concession Address).* Those who love [America} and love her people want to serve as President. (Major premise). I love this country and its people. (Minor premise). I want(ed) to serve as

President. (Conclusion)

- "It is quite recent history, Lord Randolph was Chancellor of the Exchequer, Lord Salisbury was Prime Minister, as he is now. And on this same issue of economy Lord Randolph Churchill went down -- forever. But wise words, Sir, stand the test of time. And his words were wise." -- *(From the movie Young Winston)*. Wise words stand the test of time. (Major premise). [Lord Randolph Churchill's] words were wise (Minor premise). [Lord Randolph Churchill's] words will stand the test of time. (Conclusion)

CHAPTER TWENTY-EIGHT

Rhetorical Device 28 – Enumeratio

Enumeratio breaks down a simple statement and expands it into parts with emphasis on details. These details may not be necessary to be specified, but at a specific situation Enumeratio can be used to make rhetorical impact on the minds of the listeners by engaging them with the description and details.

For Example:

<u>Original</u>: I want to expand the business into overseas markets.

<u>Enumeratio</u>: I have grown up with this business and it now needs to grow beyond our current borders into the green fields of opportunity in markets away from these shores, where we can excite new customers and build further on our outstanding success so far.

<u>Original</u>: I will go to town now.

<u>Enumeratio</u>: I am going down to the station to catch the train to town where I shall go to the bank, visit the hairdresser, buy some flowers, then catch the train back so I can be here for five o'clock, just before Richard and Jane come.

<u>Other Examples</u>

- "[W]hen we allow freedom to ring, **when we let it ring from every village and every hamlet, from every state and every city,** we will be able to speed up that day when all of God's children, **black men and white men, Jews and Gentiles,**

Protestants and Catholics, will be able to join hands and sing in the words of the old Negro spiritual, 'Free at last! **Free at last! Thank God Almighty, we are free at last!**'" -- *(Martin Luther King, Jr., "I Have a Dream," August 1963)*

- "Cast down your bucket among these people who have, without strikes and labor wars, **tilled your fields, cleared your forests, builded your railroads and cities, and brought forth treasures from the bowels of the earth, and helped make possible this magnificent representation of the progress of the South.** Casting down your bucket among my people, helping and encouraging them as you are doing on these grounds, **and to education of head, hand, and heart**, you will find that they will buy your surplus land, **make blossom the waste places in your fields, and run your factories.**" -- *(Booker T. Washington, "The Atlanta Compromise Address," September 1895)*

- "We say that if America has entered the war to make the world safe for democracy, she must first make democracy safe in America. How else is the world to take America seriously, **when democracy at home is daily being outraged, free speech suppressed, peaceable assemblies broken up by overbearing and brutal gangsters in uniform; when free press is curtailed and every independent opinion gagged.**" -- *(Emma Goldman, address to the jury during the Anti-Conscription trial in New York City, July 1917)*

- "Much will be said about my father the man, **the storyteller, the lover of costume parties, a practical joker, the accomplished painter.** He was **a lover of everything French: cheese, wine,** and women. He was **a mountain climber, navigator, skipper, tactician, airplane pilot, rodeo rider, ski jumper, dog lover, and all-around adventurer.** Our family vacations left us all injured and exhausted. He was **a dinner table debater and devil's advocate.** He was **an Irishman, and a proud member of the Democratic Party.**" -- *(Ted Kennedy, Jr., Eulogy for Ted Kennedy, Sr.)*

- "It is true that this international union is a strong, militant organization. This **international union is comprised of 17 trade divisions, an executive board of 15 individuals, 13 Vice Presidents....**" -- *(Jimmy Hoffa, 1962 Address at Harvard University)*
- "But, I think that any **ontological history of our selves has** to analyze **three sets of relations: our relations to truth; our relations to obligations; our relations to ourselves and to the others.**" -- *(Michel Foucault, UC Berkeley Lecture "The Culture of the Self")*
- "Together, Kennedy/Kerry have opposed the very weapons systems that won the Cold War and that are now winning the war on terror. The B-1 bomber, **that Senator Kerry opposed**, dropped 40% of the bombs in the first six months of [Operation] Enduring Freedom. The B-2 bomber, **that Senator Kerry opposed**, delivered air strikes against the Taliban in Afghanistan and Hussein's command post in Iraq. The F-14A Tomcats, **that Senator Kerry opposed**, shot down Khadafi's Libyan MIGs over the Gulf of Sidra. The modernized F-14D, **that Senator Kerry opposed**, delivered missile strikes against Tora Bora. The Apache helicopter, **that Senator Kerry opposed**, took out those Republican Guard tanks in Kuwait in the Gulf War. The F-15 Eagles, **that Senator Kerry opposed**, flew cover over our Nation's Capital and this very city after 9/11." -- *(Zell Miller, 2004 Republican National Convention Address)*
- "For the first time in history, people of Jewish, Catholic, and Protestant faiths are standing side by side and working in closest cooperation for the great common cause. The **seven organizations included in the campaign -- namely, the Young Men's Christian Association, the Young Women's Christian Association, the National Catholic War Council, the Jewish Welfare Board, the War Camp Community Service, the American Library Association, and the Salvation Army --** are authorized by the Secretary of War and the Secretary of the Navy to work for the soldiers and [unintelligible] in and near

the camp." -- *(John D. Rockefeller, Jr., United War Work Campaign Address)*

- "Brian was an amazing man. And I say that not just because he was family. Many people thought he was almost super human. After his death, we visited his former duty stations in Arizona. Each time we met one of his fellow agents, they spoke of how impressed they were him. He was what we expect in our brothers and sons: a **strong, competitive, handsome, courageous, funny, and incredibly patriotic American."** -- *(Robert Heyer, Statement to Congress on Border Patrol Agent Brian A. Terry)*

- "The Equal Rights Amendment was first introduced into Congress in 1923. It was born in the era of women's suffrage amendment. I'll recite it for you in case you don't know it by heart. It **says, 'Equality of life under the law shall not be denied or abridged by the United States or by any State on account of sex.' Section II says 'Congress will have the power to enforce by appropriate legislation the provisions of this Article.' And Section III has it going into effect within two years."** -- *(Phyllis Schlafly, The ERA -- is there a future?)*

- "These abuses have continued because, for too long, the history of women has been a history of silence. Even today, there are those who are trying to silence our words. But the voices of this conference and of the women at Huairou must be heard loudly and clearly: **It is a violation of human rights** when babies are denied food, or drowned, or suffocated, or their spines broken, simply because they are born girls. **It is a violation of human rights** when women and girls are sold into the slavery of prostitution for human greed -- and the kinds of reasons that are used to justify this practice should no longer be tolerated. **It is a violation of human rights** when women are doused with gasoline, set on fire, and burned to death because their marriage dowries are deemed too small. **It is a violation of human rights** when individual women are raped in their own communities and when thousands of women are subjected to rape as a tactic or prize of war. **It is a violation of human rights** when a leading cause of death worldwide among women ages 14 to 44 is the violence they are subjected to in their own homes by their own relatives. **It is a violation of human rights** when young girls are brutalized by the painful and degrading practice of genital mutilation. **It is a violation of human rights** when women are denied the right to plan their own families, and that includes being forced to have abortions or being sterilized against their will. -- *(Hillary Clinton, Women's Rights are Human Rights)*

- "Since our founding, American Muslims have enriched the United States. They have **fought in our wars**; they have **served in our government**; they have **stood for civil rights**; they have **started businesses**; they have **taught at our universities**; they've **excelled in our sports arenas**; they've won **Nobel Prizes, built our tallest building**, and **lit the Olympic Torch**." -- *(Barack Obama, Speech at Cairo University)*

- "The terrorist threat to our nation did not emerge on September 11th, 2001. Long before that day, radical, freedom-hating terrorists declared war on America and on the civilized world: **the attack on the Marine barracks in Lebanon in 1983, the hijacking of the Achille Lauro in 1985, the rise of al-Qaida and the bombing of the World Trade Center in 1993, the attacks on American installations in Saudi Arabia in 1995 and 1996, the East Africa [embassy] bombings of 1998, the attack on the USS Cole in 2000.** These and other atrocities were part of a sustained, systematic campaign to spread devastation and chaos and to murder innocent Americans." -- *(Condoleezza Rice - 9/11 Commission Hearing Statement)*

CHAPTER TWENTY-NINE

Rhetorical Device 29 – Epanalepsis

Epanalepsis is the repetition of an initial word, set of words or clause with intervening words for emphasis to a specific point in the sentence with an objective of creating rhetorical impact. As the beginning and end are the two positions which can be used for stronger emphasis, therefore, sometimes the repetition occurs at both these places.

Examples

- **Water** alone dug this giant canyon; yes, just plain **water**.
- **To report** that your committee is still investigating the matter is to tell me that you have nothing **to report**.
- **The king** is dead, long live **the king**.
- **Severe** to his servants, to his children **severe**.
- They **bowed down** to him rather, because he was all of these things, and then again he was all of these things because the town **bowed down**. — *(Zora Neale Hurston, Their Eyes Were Watching God)*
- **Beloved** is mine; she is **Beloved**.
- **Blow** winds and crack your cheeks! Rage, **blow**! —*Shakespeare, King Lear, 3.2.1*
- **Nice** to see you, to see you, **nice**. — *(Bruce Forsyth)*
- **There's a girl in the garden. In the garden there's a girl.** — *(Shaun of The Dead)*

- "A **minimum wage** that is not a livable wage can never be **a minimum wage**." *(Ralph Nader)*
- "In times like these, it is helpful to remember that there have always been times like these." *(Paul Harvey)*
- "The time must come. **It's enough**—enough to go to cemeteries, enough to weep for orphans—**it's enough**. There must come a moment, a moment of bringing people together." *(Elie Wiesel, Speech at Buchenwald Concentration Camp, 4 June 2009)*
- "Romans, countrymen, and lovers, **hear** me for my cause, and be silent, that you may **hear**. **Believe** me for mine honor, and have respect to mine honor, that you may **believe**." *(Brutus in William Shakespeare's Julius Caesar)*
- "Don't turn away from the truth. Don't turn away from your conscience. Please don't ignore the law; no, embrace that higher principle for which the law was meant to serve. **Justice**—that's all I ask—**justice**." *(Denzel Washington in The Hurricane - 1999)*
- "In **times like these**, it is helpful to remember that there have always been **times like these**." — *(Paul Harvey)*
- "**Believe** not all you can hear, tell not all you **believe**." — *(Native American proverb)*
- "**A lie** begets **a lie**." — *(English proverb)*
- "**To each** the boulders that have **fallen to each**." *(Robert Frost, "Mending Wall")*
- "**Next time** there won't be a **next time**." -- *(Phil Leotardo in The Sopranos)*
- "**He is noticeable for nothing** in the world except for the markedness by which he is **noticeable for nothing**." -- *(Edgar Allan Poe, "The Literati of New York City." Godey's Lady's Book, Sep. 1846)*
- "Possessing what we still were unpossessed by, **Possessed** by what we now no more **possessed**." -- *(Robert Frost, "The Gift Outright")*
- "**The man who did the waking** buys the man who was sleeping a drink; the man who was sleeping drinks it while listening to a proposition from **the man who did the waking**." -- *(Jack*

Sparrow, The Pirates of the Caribbean)

- "**We know nothing of one another**, nothing. Smiley mused. However closely we live together, at whatever time of day or night we sound the deepest thoughts in one another, we know nothing." -- *(John le Carré, Call for the Dead, 1961)*
- "But I ain't goin' no 10,000 miles to help murder and kill other poor people. **If I wanna die**, I'll die right here, right now fightin' you -- **if I wanna die**." -- *(Delivered by Will Smith from the movie Ali)*
- "The time must come. **It's enough** -- enough to go to cemeteries, enough to weep for oceans -- **it's enough**." -- *(Elie Wiesel, Speech at Buchenwald Concentration Camp)*
- "**Control**, control, you must learn **control**." -- *(From the movie The Empire Strikes Back)*
- "A **minimum wage** that is not a livable wage can never be a **minimum wage**." -- *(Ralph Nader)*
- "My name is Robert Neville. I'm a survivor living in New York City. I am broadcasting on all AM frequencies. If you are out there, **if anyone is out there**, I can provide food, I can provide shelter, I can provide security -- **if there's anybody out there**." -- *(Delivered by Will Smith from the movie, I Am Legend)*
- "I ask you to consider the evidence. Don't turn away from the truth. Don't turn away from your conscience. Please, don't ignore the law. No, embrace that higher principle for which the law was meant to serve: **Justice** -- that's all I ask -- **justice**." -- *(Delivered by Denzel Washington from the movie The Hurricane)*

CHAPTER THIRTY

Rhetorical Device 30 – Epistrophe

Epistrophe is an emphatic device which is used to create rhetorical impact by the repetition of a word or set of words at the end of successive phrases, clauses or sentences. It creates a rhyming pattern which captures the attention of the listener.

<u>**Examples**</u>

- "A day may come when the courage of men fails, when we forsake our friends and break all bonds of fellowship, **but it is not this day**. An hour of woes and shattered shields, when the age of men comes crashing down! **But it is not this day**! This day we fight!" -- *(Viggo Mortensen as Aragorn in The Lord of the Rings: The Return of the King, 2003)*

- "Don't you ever talk about **my friends**! You don't know any of **my friends**. You don't look at any of **my friends**. And you certainly wouldn't condescend to speak to any of **my friends**." -- *(Judd Nelson as John Bender in The Breakfast Club, 1985)*

- "For no government is better than the men who compose it, and I want **the best**, and we need **the best**, and we deserve **the best**." -- *(Senator John F. Kennedy, speech at Wittenberg College, Oct. 17, 1960)*

- "It is rather for us the living, we here be dedicated to the great task remaining before us--that from these honored dead we take increased devotion to that cause for which they here gave the last full measure of devotion--that we here highly resolve that these dead shall not have died in vain, that this nation shall have a new birth of freedom, and that government of **the people**, by **the people**, for **the people** shall not perish from the earth." -- *(Abraham Lincoln, The Gettysburg Address, Nov. 19, 1863)*

- What lies behind **us** and what lies before **us** are tiny compared to what lies within **us**." — *(Emerson)*

- We are born to **sorrow**, pass our time in **sorrow**, end our days in **sorrow**.

- **Barack Obama:** "For when we have faced down impossible odds, when we've been told we're not ready or that we shouldn't try or that we can't, generations of Americans have responded with a simple creed that sums up the spirit of a people: Yes, we can. Yes, we can. **Yes, we can.** "It was a creed written into the founding documents that declared the destiny of a nation: **Yes, we can.** "It was whispered by slaves and abolitionists as they blazed a trail towards freedom through the darkest of nights: **Yes, we can.** "It was sung by immigrants as they struck out from distant shores and pioneers who pushed westward against an unforgiving wilderness: **Yes, we can.** "It was the call of workers who organized, women who reached for the ballot, a president who chose the moon as our new frontier, and a king who took us to the mountaintop and pointed the way to the promised land: **Yes, we can**, to justice and equality. "Yes, we can, to opportunity and prosperity. Yes, we can heal this nation. Yes, we can repair this world. **Yes, we can.**" -- *(Senator Barack Obama, speech following a primary loss in New Hampshire, Jan. 8, 2008)*

- Where affections bear rule, their reason is **subdued**, honesty is **subdued**, good will is **subdued**, and all things else that withstand evil, forever are **subdued**. — *(Thomas Wilson)*

- When I was a **child**, I spoke as a **child**, I understood as a **child**, I thought as a **child**. But when I became a man, I put away childish things.

- "There is no Negro **problem**. There is no Southern **problem**. There is no Northern **problem**. There is only an American

problem." -- *(Lyndon B. Johnson in "We Shall Overcome")*

- "What lies behind us and what lies before us are tiny compared to what lies within us." — *(Ralph Waldo Emerson)*
- "The time for the healing of the wounds **has come**. The moment to bridge the chasms that divides us **has come**."—*(Nelson Mandela)*
- "The minister who has been called **by God**, ordained **by God**, appointed **by God**, and anointed **by God**, is assumed guilty until proven innocent."—*(Ravi Zacharias)*
- The time is **now**, the need is **now**, we must act, **now**!
- "Where **now**? Who **now**? When **now**?" – *(Samuel Beckett, The Unnamable)*
- "There is nothing wrong **with America** that cannot be cured by what is right **with America**." – *(Bill Clinton)*
- Are we downhearted? - **No we are not**! Are we defeated? - **No we are not**! Are we depressed? - **No we are not**!
- "You have the luxury of not knowing what I know -- that Santiago's death, while tragic, probably saved **lives**, and my existence, while grotesque and incomprehensible to you, saves **lives**." -- *(Jack Nicholson from the movie A Few Good Men)*
- "Now I want you to remember that no bastard ever won a war by dying **for his country**. He won it by making the other poor dumb bastard die **for his country**." -- *(Delivered by George C. Scott from the movie Patton)*

CHAPTER THIRTY-ONE

Rhetorical Device 31 – Epitheton

Epitheton is the attribute added with a person or thing which describes the quality or characteristic with an objective of better representation. This is achieved sometimes by the simple addition of a descriptive adjective and sometimes through a descriptive or metaphorical apposition. (e.g., "fun ride," "bad omen," "cheerful giver," "good and decent man")

<u>**Examples**</u>

- Sitting by his side, I watched the **peaceful dawn.**
- My **careful steps** reached the attic.
- Her **stifled laughter** made everybody nervous.
- In the face of such a tragedy, his **laughing happiness** seemed queer.
- I had reached a **delicate corner.**
- The **idle road** stretched for miles.
- All I can say is that he had an **honest end.**
- It was a **sweet beginning** to a tragic end.
- Her **depressing ways** ruined her mother's health.
- "Somewhere today, a mother facing **punishing poverty** still takes the time to teach her child, scrapes together what few coins she has to send that child to school -- because she believes that a cruel world still has a place for that child's dreams." -- *(Barack Obama, Nobel Prize for Peace Lecture)*

- "And that's the foreign policy I want -- an America outside all these **entangling alliances....**" -- *(Pat Buchanan, Interview with Rush Limbaugh)*
- "Now, in this **anxious autumn** from those **heroic men**, there comes back an **answering appeal**." -- *(Dwight D. Eisenhower, 1952 Stump Speech)*
- "We stand today on one of the **strange promontories** of **human history**." -- *(Thomas E. Dewey, 1944 Eve of Election Address)*
- "I will give the people a vision of Rome and they'll love me for it. And they'll soon forget the **tedious sermonizing** of a **few dry old men**." -- *(Delivered by Joaquin Phoenix from the movie Gladiator)*
- "For if this book is a joke, it is a joke against me. It recounts my **elephantine adventures** in pursuit of the obvious." -- *(G.K. Chesterton, Orthodoxy)*
- "I accept this award on behalf of a civil rights movement which is moving with determination and a **majestic scorn** for risk and danger to establish a reign of freedom and a rule of justice." -- *(Martin Luther King, Nobel Peace Prize Acceptance)*
- "Western European nations show their determination to resist aggression. All could acquire an **unbreakable strength** if bundled together." -- *(Bernard Baruch, On the Cold War)*

CHAPTER THIRTY-TWO

Rhetorical Device 32 - Epizeuxis

An epizeuxis is the repetition of words in immediate succession and with no words in between, for intensity or emphasis. This creates rhetorical impact by intentionally repeating words for extra emphasis on the idea.

<u>Examples</u>

- "Never, never, never quit." (*Winston Churchill*)
- "Location, location, location." (*Common phrase tied to real estate*)
- "The horror, the horror" (*Kurtz in Heart of Darkness*)
- "No, no, no!" (*Margaret Thatcher*)
- "O horror, horror, horror." (*Macbeth*)
- "Words, words, words." (*Hamlet*)
- "Rain, rain, rain, rain, rain." (*Kay*)
- "Education, education, education." (*Tony Blair*)
- "Simplicity, simplicity, simplicity!" (*Henry David Thoreau in Walden*)
- **Alone, alone**, all all alone,
- Alone on a **wide, wide** sea".
- (Samuel Coleridge in The Rime of the Ancient Mariner)
- Round here we stay up **very, very, very, very** late".
- (*Counting Crows in Round Here*)
- "I undid the lantern cautiously--oh, so **cautiously--cautiously**." -- (*Edgar Allan Poe, "The Tell-Tale Heart," 1843*)

- "There's little in taking or giving, There's little in water or wine; **This living, this living, this living,** Was never a project of mine." -- *(Dorothy Parker, "Coda")*
- "Bad, **fast! Fast! Fast!** Last night I cut the light off in my bedroom, hit the switch and was in the bed before the room was dark." -- *(Muhammad Ali)*
- "**It's a twister! It's a twister!**" -- *(Zeke in The Wizard of Oz, 1939)*
- "**Strong men also cry. Strong men also cry.**"
- *(The Big Lebowski in The Big Lebowski, 1998)*
- "**Give me a break! Give me a break**! Break me off a piece of that Kit Kat bar!" -- *(Advertising jingle)*
- "I'm **shocked, shocked** to find that gambling is going on in here!" -- *(Captain Renault in Casablanca, 1942)*
- "For a nation which has an almost evil reputation for **bustle, bustle, bustle,** and **rush, rush, rush**, we spend an enormous amount of time standing around in line in front of windows, just waiting." -- *(Robert Benchley, "Back in Line." Benchley--or Else! 1947)*
- "Oh you need **fluff, fluff, fluff**, To make a fluffer nutter, Marshmallow fluff and lots of peanut butter. First you **spread, spread, spread**, Your bread with peanut butter, Add marshmallow fluff and have a fluffernutter." *(Advertising jingle)*
- "The rich nations and the poor nations have different responsibilities, but one responsibility we all have -- and that is action. **Action, action, action**. The current stalemate between the developed and the developing worlds must be broken. It is time to came together in a new international agreement that can be embraced by rich and poor nations alike." -- *(Arnold Schwarzenegger, United Nations Address on Climate Change)*
- "Isn't extraordinary that the Prime Minister of our country can't even urge his Party to support his own position?! Yeah. **Weak! Weak! Weak!** -- *(Tony Blair, 1997 House of Commons exchange with Prime Minister John Major)*
- "**Warning! Warning! Warning**! Alien approaching!" -- *(From the movie Lost in Space)*

- "You wanna know what I make? I make kids wonder. I make 'em question. I make 'em criticize. I make 'em apologize -- and mean it. I make 'em **write, write, write.** And then I make 'em read. I make 'em spell: **definitely beautiful, definitely beautiful, definitely beautiful -- over and over and over again,** until they will never misspell either one of those words again." -- *(Delivered by Taylor Mali)*

- I really **hated, hated, hated** being sent to report on other people's tragedies as a part of my daily duty. -- *(Oprah Winfrey, Stanford Commencement Address)*

- "Here he is! The one and only winner of the Gemini Croquet contest! This boy is fueled, like FIRE! So start melting ladies 'cause the boy is hotter than hot. He's **Hot Hot! Hot!!**" -- *(Delivered by Chris Tucker from the movie The 5th Element)*

- "I, along with millions -- scores of millions -- of Americans, will **pray, pray, pray** for the safety of our troops." -- *(Robert C. Byrd, The Arrogance of Power)*

- "And we must build effective coalitions capable of confronting dangerous regimes like Iran and North Korea. It's time for more than just tough talk. Just like you -- probably just so tired of hearing the **talk, talk, talk.** -- *(Sarah Palin, Tea Party Convention Keynote Speech)*

CHAPTER THIRTY-THREE

Rhetorical Device 33 – Eponym

An Eponym is a word that has a source from the name of a person (living or dead), mythical character, place, item, tribe, era, discovery etc. For example, eponyms in English include **boycott, braille, camellia, chauvinist, dahlia, diesel, dunce, gardenia, gerrymander, guillotine, hooligan, leotard, lynch, magnolia, ohm, pasteurize, poinsettia, praline, quixotic, ritzy, sequoia, shrapnel, silhouette, volt, watt, and zeppelin.**

<u>Examples</u>

- **Sandwich**: named after John Montagu, the Fourth Earl of Sandwich (1718–1792), a British politician.
- **Cardigan**: a knitted garment, such as a sweater or jacket, that opens down the front. Named after the Seventh Earl of Cardigan, James Thomas Brudenell (1797–1868), a British army officer.
- "Let's not **Rumsfeld** Afghanistan." -- (*Senator Lindsey Graham, quoted in Time magazine, Aug. 24, 2009*)
- **Saxophone**: named after Sax, the surname of a 19th-century instrument-making family in Belgium.
- "Alton Brown can fill an entire episode on popcorn, teaching you how to **MacGyver** a nifty, cheap popper (hint: a stainless-steel bowl and some perforated foil)." -- (*Entertainment Weekly, Aug. 14, 2009*)

- "The crowd parted reluctantly, and [Lance Armstrong] glided off, **Batmanning** through the crowd toward the start line." -- *(Daniel Coyle, Lance Armstrong's War. HarperCollins, 2005)*
- An earthworm is the **Hercules** of the soil.
- With a bow and arrow, Kathy is a real **Diana**. [Diana was goddess of the moon, of the hunt, and of chastity.]
- Those of us who cannot become a **Ulysses** and see the world must trust our knowledge to picture books and descriptions. [Ulysses was a hero in the Trojan War as well as a wanderer afterwards.]
- The wisdom of a **Solomon** was needed to figure out the actions of the appliance marketplace this quarter.
- "Americans now nibble their way through two billion popsicles a year; their favourite flavour is a **Jaggeresque** red cherry." -- *(Oliver Thring, "Consider Ice Lollies." The Guardian, July 27, 2010)*
- Is he smart? Why, the man is an **Einstein**. Has he suffered? This poor Job can tell you himself.
- That little **Caesar** is fooling nobody. He knows he is no Patrick Henry.
- When it comes to watching girls, Fred is a regular **Argus**.
- You think your boyfriend is tight. I had a date with **Scrooge** himself last night.
- We all must realize that **Uncle Sam** is not supposed to be **Santa Claus**.

CHAPTER THIRTY-FOUR

Rhetorical Device 34 – Euphemismos

Euphemismos is the usage of polite expression in place of words or expression which could be considered as harsh or offensive in normal language. Euphemism means to replace a milder, indirect or vague word for the one which could be considered as offensive, blunt or harsh and are unpleasant to hear. For example, usage of **"passed away"** in place of **"died"**.

Examples

- **Ethnic cleansing** instead of **genocide**
- **Negative patient outcome** instead of **dead**
- **Relocation center** instead of **prison camp**
- **Collateral damage** instead of **accidental deaths**
- **Letting someone go** instead of **firing someone**
- **Passed away instead of died**
- **Correctional facility** instead of **jail**
- **Departed** instead of **died**
- **Differently-abled** instead of **handicapped or disabled**
- **Put to sleep** instead of **euthanize**
- **Pregnancy termination** instead of **abortion**
- **On the streets** instead of **homeless**
- Instead of **Secretary** use **executive assistant, personal assistant**
- Instead of **School** use **academy, conservatory**
- Instead of **Boss** use **manager, supervisor, director**

- Instead of **Garbage Collector** use **sanitation worker, waste disposal worker**
- Instead of **Janitor** use **caretaker, custodian, warden**
- **Comfort woman** instead of **prostitute**
- **Adult entertainment** instead of **pornography**
- **Use the rest room** instead of **go to the bathroom**
- **Economical with the truth** instead of **liar**
- **Between jobs** instead of **unemployed**
- **Domestic engineer** instead of **maid**
- **Sanitation engineer** instead of **garbage man**
- **Vertically-challenged** instead of **short**
- **Adult beverages** instead of **beer or liquor**
- **Big-boned** instead of **heavy or overweight**
- **Chronologically-challenged** instead of **late**

CHAPTER THIRTY-FIVE

Rhetorical Device 35 – Exemplum

Exemplum is the figure of speech in which amplification is created using an example, brief story or anecdote, small narration which could be real or fictitious, with an objective to illustrate a claim, idea, quotation or moral point.

For Example:

- You should give me you full support, **just like Simon here.**
- **Many people have learned to do this.** You can too.

Examples

- Bugs Bunny eats carrots and I think they make him happy. Eat up!
- How could we do it out here? **The Greeks and Persians of old did not need great machines but used their ingenuity.** All we need is our minds and the resources around us.
- Let me give you an example. In the early 1920's in Germany, the government let the printing presses turn out endless quantities of paper money, and soon, instead of 50-pfennige postage stamps, denominations up to 50 billion marks were being issued.
- "Scientists can do more, but we've got to give them the chance. And that means more funding for research. **Right now, for example, about a quarter million Americans have a spinal**

chord injury." -- *(Christopher Reeve, 1996 Democratic National Convention Address)*

- "There are other great lessons too. **For example, there are hundreds of thousands of Americans that take part in this game annually, and yet it is completely uninhibited by either racial or social barriers."** -- *(Vince Lombardi)*

- "We have tried since the year nineteen hundred and thirty-five to educate our local unions to the acceptance of area-wide contracts, with membership as large as international unions have in the entire United States. **As an example, we have 165,000 members in New York city; we have 147,000 in Chicago; we have 140,000 in Los Angeles."** -- *(Jimmy Hoffa, 1962 Address at Harvard University)*

- "Arachnids from all three groups possess various strengths which help them in their constant search for food. **For example, The Delana spider, family Sparassidae, has the ability to jump to catch its prey."** -- *(From the movie Spiderman)*

- "All this stuff you've heard about America not wanting to fight, wanting to stay out of the war, is a lot of horse dung. Americans, traditionally, love to fight. All real Americans love the sting of battle. **When you were kids, you all admired the champion marble shooter, the fastest runner, the big league ball players, the toughest boxers.** Americans love a winner and will not tolerate a loser. Americans play to win all the time. Now, I wouldn't give a hoot in hell for a man who lost and laughed." -- *(Delivered by George C. Scott from the movie Patton)*

- "I've come to understand that a cultural war is raging across our land. **For example, I marched for civil rights with Dr. King in 1963. But when I told an audience last year that white pride is just as valid as black pride or red pride or anyone else's pride, they called me a racist."** -- *(Charleton Heston, Winning the Cultural War)*

CHAPTER THIRTY-SIX

Rhetorical Device 36 – Expletive

Expletive is a word, expression or a short phrase, which is utilized for emphasis to the words in immediate proximity, generally interrupting the normal syntax of the sentence. Typical examples include: certainly, remarkably, indeed, you know, of course, to be sure, in any event, in effect, you see, clearly, in fact, I suppose, I hope, I think.

Examples

- "**It is** easy when we are in prosperity to give advice to the afflicted." -- *(Aeschylus)*
- "**There are** three kinds of lies: lies, damned lies, and statistics." -- *(Benjamin Disraeli)*
- "**There are** only two ways to live your life. One is as though nothing is a miracle. The other is as though everything is a miracle." -- *(Albert Einstein)*
- "I would like, **if I may**, to take you on a strange journey." -- *(From the movie Rocky Horror Picture Show)*
- "The strength of America's response, **please understand**, flows from the principles upon which we stand." -- *(Rudy Giuliani, 9/11 Speech to the United Nations General Assembly)*
- "We do **indeed** and have discriminated against women..." -- *(Betty Friedan, Women -- Do we dare not discriminate)*

- "The minimum wage, **I might add**, today is far less than it was in 1960 and 1970 in terms of purchasing power." -- *(Ralph Nader, 2000 NAACP Address)*
- "It would be fitting and good, **I think**, if, on each inaugural day in future years, it should be declared a day of prayer." -- *(Ronald Reagan, First Inaugural Address)*

CHAPTER THIRTY-SEVEN

Rhetorical Device 37 - Hyperbaton

Hyperbaton is used to create rhetorical impact by deviating from normal or logical word order, in the sentence, to create a differently structured form to convey the same meaning for producing an effect. This is achieved by separating the normally associated words to make language take a sudden turn or interruption.

Examples

- It was a long operation but successful.
- Let's go on a cooler day and less busy.
- So many pages will require a longer staple, heavy-duty style.
- In this room there sit twenty (though I will not name them) distinguished people.
- We will not, from this house, under any circumstances, be evicted.
- Sandy, after a long struggle, all the way across the lake, finally swam to shore.
- "Object there was none. Passion there was none. I loved the old man." -- *(Edgar Allan Poe, "The Tell-Tale Heart")*
- "Some rise by sin, and some by virtue fall." -- *(Escalus in William Shakespeare's Measure for Measure, Act II, scene one)*
- "And a small cabin build there, of clay and wattles made" -- *(W. B. Yeats, "The Lake Isle of Innisfree")*

- "One swallow does not a summer make, nor one fine day." -- *(Aristotle)*
- From his seat on the bench he saw the girl content-content with the promise that she could ride on the train again next week.
- She had a personality indescribable.
- His was a countenance sad.
- His was a countenance friendly.
- These are rumors strange
- Welcome to our home comfortable.
- That is a story amazing.

CHAPTER THIRTY-EIGHT

Rhetorical Device 38 – Hyperbole

Hyperbole achieves rhetorical impact through exaggeration by using an extravagant phrase or statement to evoke deep feelings, emotional response or strong impression. But, this expression is not meant to be taken literally as its only purpose is the emphasis on the idea. Media and advertising industry often uses it to create media hype. It is often used in poetry and even in casual speech for humor.

Examples of hyperbole are:

- They ran like **greased lightning**.
- He's got **tons of money**.
- Her brain is the **size of a pea**.
- He is **older than the hills**.
- I will **die** if she asks me to dance.
- She is as **big as an elephant!**
- I'm so hungry I could **eat a horse**.
- I have told you a **million times** not to lie!

Other Examples

- The **whole world** was staring at me
- It took him **two seconds** to drive here
- His teeth were **blinding white**
- I don't have **two cents** to rub together

- I am so tired I could **sleep for a year**
- The **blue bells of the sky** were **broken by the wind**
- The **mountain of paperwork** weighed heavily on the teacher's desk
- The ancient castle was so big that it **took a week** to walk from one end to the other
- Sarah's hair was a **velvet black curtain** against her back
- The engagement ring he gave her was so small that a **magnifying glass** was needed to see it
- He was so skinny that when he turned sideways it looked like **a tin sheet**
- My mother's lecture on good manners lasted **two weeks** one afternoon
- You snore louder than a **freight train**
- I have seen this river so wide it had **only one bank**
- That joke is so old, the last time I heard it I was **riding on a dinosaur**
- If he talks to me in front of everyone, I will **die of embarrassment**
- Our new school is large enough to have its **own zip code**
- My backpack **weighs a ton!**
- I'm so busy trying to accomplish **ten million things** at once
- She is a **hundred feet tall**
- He is as big as a **grown elephant!**
- His smile was a **mile wide**
- Her eyes were as **wide as saucers**
- It's **raining cats and dogs**
- It is going to take a **zillion years** to get through Medical School
- There are **millions** of other things to do
- Running faster than the **speed of light**
- It took **light years** for this to work
- I waited in line for **centuries**
- I had to walk fifteen miles up-hill both ways, in **snow five feet deep**

- "So first of all, let me assert my firm belief that **the only thing we have to fear is fear itself."** -- *(Franklin Delano Roosevelt, First Inaugural Address)*
- "The chamber is celebrating an important milestone this week: your 70th anniversary. I **remember the day you started."** -- *(Ronald Reagan)*
- **"The only place where democracy comes before work is in the dictionary."** -- *(Ralph Nader, 2000 NAACP Address)*
- **"Why you got scars and knots on your head from the top of your head to the bottom of your feet. And every one of those scars is evidence against the American white man."** -- *(Malcolm X)*

CHAPTER THIRTY-NINE

Rhetorical Device 39 – Hypophora

Speakers utilize Hypophora to create rhetorical impact by raising one or more questions and then immediately answering them, usually at some length. Generally, the question is raised at the beginning and is the answered during the course of the speech. It can also be used to present or introduce a new area of discussion.

<u>Examples</u>:

- "And how'd you get that [becoming King], eh? By exploiting the workers! By hanging on to outdated imperialist dogma which perpetuates the economic and social differences in our society." --*(Monty Python, Monty Python and the Holy Grail 1975)*
- "What should young people do with their lives today? Many things, obviously. But the most daring thing is to create stable communities in which the terrible disease of loneliness can be cured." -- *(Kurt Vonnegut)*
- "What makes a king out of a slave? Courage! What makes the flag on the mast to wave? Courage! What makes the elephant charge his tusk in the misty mist, or the dusky dusk? What makes the muskrat guard his musk? Courage! -- *(The Cowardly Lion in The Wizard of Oz, 1939)*
- "Do you know the difference between education and experience? Education is when you read the fine print; experience is what you get when you don't." -- *(Pete Seeger in*

Loose Talk, ed. by Linda Botts, 1980)

- "You ask, what is our policy? I will say it is to wage war, by sea, land, and air, with all our might and all the strength that God can give us; to wage war against a monstrous tyranny, never surpassed in the dark, lamentable catalog of human crime. That is our policy. "You ask, what is our aim? I can answer in one word: Victory. Victory at all costs, victory in spite of all terror; victory, however long and hard the road may be, for without victory, there is no survival."-- *(Winston Churchill, 13 May 1940)*
- "What is George Bush doing about our economic problems? He has raised taxes on the people driving pickup trucks and lowered taxes on the people riding in limousines." -- *(William Jefferson Clinton, 1992 DNC Acceptance Address)*
- "Just what are the problems in Los Angeles in those households in which a mother and father are both resident? How may a national ethos be ignited on the subject of single parent procreation? An attitude has to evolve that begins with solemnizing marriage." -- *(William F. Buckley, Reflections on Current Contentions)*
- "What shall Cordelia speak? Love, and be silent." -- *(Cordelia in King Lear by William Shakespeare)*
- "You boil it all down, what does a man really need? Just a smoke and a cup of coffee." -- *(Sterling Hayden as Johnny Guitar in Johnny Guitar, 1954)*
- "When the enemy struck on that June day of 1950, what did America do? It did what it always has done in all its times of peril. It appealed to the heroism of its youth."-- *(Dwight D. Eisenhower, I Shall Go to Korea Address)*
- "Since we have come so far, whom shall be rash enough to set limits on our future progress? Who shall say that since we have gone so far, we can go no farther? Who shall say that the American dream is ended? For myself, I believe that all we have done upon this continent is but a prelude to a future in which we shall become not only a bigger people but also a wiser people, a better people, an even greater people." -- *(Adlai Stevenson, 1953*

Stump Speech)

CHAPTER FORTY

Rhetorical Device 40 – Hypotaxis

In Hypotaxis the clauses in the sentences are subordinated to one another for connection or relationship, which carry different weights, to express individual but related thought within the sentence. The subordinate clauses give precise meaning to the main idea expressed by the sentence. It is used as a tool for logical argument for persuasion.

Relationships you can show include:

- Cause-and-effect: A leads to B
- Conditional: If A then B
- Set-membership: A is a part of B

Hypotaxis is the opposite of Parataxis
For Example

- I had a drink because I was thirsty.
- When I go out, I feel happy.
- If you have passed the test you can drive by yourself.

<u>Other Examples</u>

- They asked the question because they were curious.

- If a person observing an unusual or unfamiliar object concludes that it is probably a spaceship from another world, he can readily adduce that the object is reacting to his presence or actions when in reality there is absolutely no cause-effect relationship. – *(Philip Klass)*
- While I am in the world, I am the light of the world. – *(John 9:5)*
- "One December morning near the end of the year when snow was falling moist and heavy for miles all around, so that the earth and the sky were indivisible, Mrs. Bridge emerged from her home and spread her umbrella." -- *(Evan S. Connell, Mrs. Bridge, 1959)*
- "Holmes, a thrice-wounded officer of the Twentieth Massachusetts Volunteers, knew whereof he spoke, certainly. The passage [above] is drawn up like lines of battle, 'If' clauses (the protasis) that one has to pass one-by-one before reaching the 'Then' clause (the apodosis). The 'syntax' is, in the literal sense of the Greek, a line of battle. The sentence . . . seems to map a series of Civil War skirmish lines. This is hypotactic arrangement for certain." -- *(Richard A. Lanham, Analyzing Prose, 2nd ed. Continuum, 2003)*
- "Let the reader be introduced to Joan Didion, upon whose character and doings much will depend of whatever interest these pages may have, as she sits at her writing table in her own room in her own house on Welbeck Street." -- *(Joan Didion, Democracy, 1984)*
- "When I was around nine or ten I wrote a play which was directed by a young, white schoolteacher, a woman, who then took an interest in me, and gave me books to read, and, in order to corroborate my theatrical bent, decided to take me to see what she somewhat tactlessly referred to as 'real' plays." -- *(James Baldwin, "Notes of a Native Son," 1955)*
- "After the lions had returned to their cages, creeping angrily through the chutes, a little bunch of us drifted away and into an open doorway nearby, where we stood for a while in semi-darkness watching a big brown circus horse go harumphing

around the practice ring." -- *(E. B. White, "The Ring of Time")*

- "Considering how common illness is, how tremendous the spiritual change that it brings, how astonishing when the lights of health go down, the undiscovered countries that are then disclosed, what wastes and deserts of the soul a slight attack of influenza brings to view, what precipices and lawns sprinkled with bright flowers a little rise of temperature reveals, what ancient and obdurate oaks are uprooted in us by the act of sickness, how we go down into the pit of death and feel the waters of annihilation close above our heads and wake thinking to find ourselves in the presence of the angels and the harpers when we have a tooth out and come to the surface in the dentist's arm-chair and confuse his 'Rinse the mouth--rinse the mouth' with the greeting of the Deity stooping from the floor of Heaven to welcome us--when we think of this, as we are so frequently forced to think of it, it becomes strange indeed that illness has not taken its place with love and battle and jealousy among the prime themes of literature." -- *(Virginia Woolf, "On Being Ill." New Criterion, Jan. 1926)*

- "If you have advanced in line and have seen ahead of you the spot you must pass where the rifle bullets are striking; if you have ridden at night at a walk toward the blue line of fire at the dead angle of Spottsylvania, where for twenty-four hours the soldiers were fighting on the two sides of an earthwork, and in the morning the dead and dying lay piled in a row six deep, and as you rode you heard the bullets splashing in the mud and earth about you; if you have been in the picket-line at night in a black and unknown wood, have heard the splat of the bullets upon the trees, and as you moved have felt your foot slip upon a dead man's body; if you have had a blind fierce gallop against the enemy, with your blood up and a pace that left no time for fear-- if, in short, as some, I hope many, who hear me, have known, you have known the vicissitudes of terror and triumph in war; you know that there is such a thing as the faith I spoke of." -- *(Oliver Wendell Holmes, Jr., "The Soldier's Faith." Harvard University, May*

30, 1895)

Rhetorical Device 41 -Litotes

Litotes is an understatement in which a positive statement is expressed by negating or denial of its opposite expressions, principally via double negatives, for rhetorical effect. Litotes is an understatement which is deliberate for emphasis. Context is also an important element to interpret the meaning of negation.

For example, rather than saying that something is **attractive** (or even very attractive), one might merely say it is "**not unattractive**".

- **Not bad** instead of **Good**
- **No ordinary city** instead of **a very impressive city**
- **Not as young** instead of **old**
- **Not wrong** instead of **correct**
- **Not unlike** instead of **like**
- **Not that good looking** instead of **ugly**

Examples

- He is **not unaware** of what you said behind his back.
- This is **no minor** matter.
- The weather is **not unpleasant** at all.
- She's **no doll**.
- That was **no small** issue.
- The city is **not unclean**.

- Rap videos with dancers in them are **not uncommon**
- Running a marathon in under two hours is **no small** accomplishment.
- She's **no idiot**.
- That's **not a meager** sum.
- You're **not doing badly**.
- That's **no mean feat**.
- She's **not a bad** writer at all.
- Hitting that telephone pole certainly didn't do your car **any good**.
- He who examines his own self **will not long remain** ignorant of his failings.
- "The grave's a fine a **private place**
- They **aren't the happiest** couple around.
- He's **not the ugliest** fellow around!
- She's **not the brightest** girl in the class.
- The food is **not bad**.
- It is **no ordinary** city.
- That sword was **not useless** to the warrior now.
- He was **not unfamiliar** with the works of Dickens.
- She is **not as young** as she was.
- You **are not wrong**.
- Einstein is **not a bad mathematician**.
- Heat waves **are not** rare in the summer.
- It **won't be easy** to find crocodiles in the dark.
- He is **not unlike** his dad.
- That's **no small** accomplishment.
- He is **not the kindest** person I've met.
- That is **no ordinary** boy.
- **But none**, I think, **do there embrace**." -- *(Andrew Marvell, "To His Coy Mistress")*
- "Now we have a refuge to go to. A refuge that the Cylons **know nothing** about! It won't be an easy journey." -- *(Battlestar Galactica, 2003)*

- "I am **not unaware** how the productions of the Grub Street brotherhood have of late years fallen under many prejudices." -- *(Jonathan Swift, A Tale of a Tub, 1704)*
- "Keep an eye on your mother whom we both **know doesn't** have both oars in the water." -- *(Jim Harrison, The Road Home. Grove Press, 1999)*
- "We made a difference. We made the city stronger, we made the city freer, and we left her in good hands. All in all, **not bad**, not bad at all." -- *(Ronald Reagan, Farewell Address to the Nation, January 20, 1989)*

CHAPTER FORTY-TWO

Rhetorical Device 42 – Metabasis

Metabasis is used for smooth transition from one subject to another through the use of a transitional statement by recalling or reminding listeners/ readers about what has been said or presented and introducing what will be said or follow.

<u>Examples</u>

- "You have heard how the proposed plan will fail; now consider how an alternative might succeed."
- Such, then, would be my diagnosis of the present condition of art. I must now, by special request, say what I think will happen to art in the future. – *(Kenneth Clark)*
- We have to this point been examining the proposal advanced by Smervits only in regard to its legal practicability; but next we need to consider the effect it would have in retarding research and development work in private laboratories.
- I have hitherto made mention of his noble enterprises in France, and now I will rehearse his worthy acts done near to Rome. – *(Peacham)*
- Now that I have made this catalogue of swindles and perversions, let me give another example of the kind of writing that they lead to. – *(George Orwell)*
- By the foregoing quotation I have shown that the language of prose may yet be well adapted to poetry; and I have previously

asserted that a large portion of the language of every good poem can in no respect differ from that of good prose. I will go further. I do not doubt that it may be safely affirmed, that there neither is, nor can be, any essential difference between the language of prose and metrical composition. – *(William Wordsworth)*

- Having thus explained a few of the reasons why I have written in verse, and why I have chosen subjects from common life, and endeavored to bring my language near to the real language of men, . . . I request the reader's permission to add a few words with reference solely to these particular poems and to some defects which will probably be found in them.

- Now that we have discussed the different kinds of cactus plants available to the landscape architect, their physical requirements for sun, soil, irrigation, and drainage, and the typical design groupings selected for residential areas, we ought to examine the architectural contexts which can best use-enhance and be enhanced by--cactus planters and gardens.

- Thus we have surveyed the state of authors as they are influenced from without, either by the frowns or favor of the great, or by the applause or censure of the critics. It remains only to consider how the people, or world in general, stand affected towards our modern penmen, and what occasion these adventurers may have of complaint or boast from their encounter with the public. – *(Anthony Ashley Cooper, Earl of Shaftesbury)*

CHAPTER FORTY-THREE

Rhetorical Device 43 – Metanoia

In Metanoia the rhetorical impact is created through correction i.e. retracting a statement or amplifying it, and then stating it in a better way. It can weaken the previous statement (idea or declaration) or strengthen it.

<u>**Examples**</u>

- This is the worst--no, the absolute worst--excuse I have heard.
- Fido was the friendliest of all St. Bernards, nay of all dogs.
- The chief thing to look for in impact sockets is hardness; no, not so much hardness as resistance to shock and shattering.
- And if I am still far from the goal, the fault is my own for not paying heed to the reminders--nay, the virtual directions--which I have had from above. – *(Marcus Aurelius)*
- Even a blind man can see, as the saying is, that poetic language gives a certain grandeur to prose, except that some writers imitate the poets quite openly, or rather they do not so much imitate them as transpose their words into their own work, as Herodotus does. – *(Demetrius)*

CHAPTER FORTY-FOUR

Rhetorical Device 44 – Metaphor

In Metaphor similarity between two different objects is identified based on a single or some common characteristics. This comparison can be hidden, implicit or implied and it is not literally applicable.

A metaphor is distinct from, but related to a simile, which is also a comparison. The primary difference is that a simile uses the word 'like' or 'as' to compare two things, while a metaphor simply suggests that the dissimilar things are the same.

For example, Sea of grief, Fishing, Broken heart, The light of my life, It's raining men, Time is a thief, He is the apple of my eye, Bubby personality, Feel blue, Fade off to sleep, Inflamed your temper, Reeks of infidelity, Rollercoaster of emotions, Stench of failure

<u>Examples</u>

- Reading that book kindled my interest in politics.
- He broke into her conversation.
- It wasn't long before their relationship turned sour.
- Time is a thief.
- My father is a rock.
- I'm not an angel, but I wouldn't behave like that.
- Harry lost his job after a heated argument with his boss.
- The committee shot her ideas down one by one.
- He swam in the sea of diamonds.

- You are my sunshine.
- He has a heart of gold.
- His head was spinning with ideas.
- His home was a prison.
- Life is a journey, purposes are destinations, means are routes, difficulties are obstacles, counselors are guides, achievements are landmarks and choices are crossroads.
- The new movie was very popular. People flocked to see it.
- A lifetime is a day, death is sleep; a lifetime is a year, death is winter.
- Life has a tendency to come back and bite you.
- Your love is an ocean
- Life is a mere dream, a fleeting shadow on a cloudy day.
- The private detective dug up enough evidence to convince the police to act.
- A light in a sea of darkness
- "Four score and seven years ago our fathers brought forth, upon this continent, a new nation, conceived in Liberty, and dedicated to the proposition that all men are created equal." - *(Abraham Lincoln, The Gettysburg Address, 1863)*
- "Memory is a crazy woman that hoards colored rags and throws away food." - *(Austin O'Malley, Keystones of Thought)*
- "Icc formed on the butler's upper slopes." - *(P.G. Wodehouse, The Color of the Woosters, 1938)*
- "But silk has nothing to do with tobacco. It's a metaphor, a metaphor that means something like, 'smooth as silk.' Somebody in an advertising agency dreamt up the name 'Silk Cut' to suggest a cigarette that wouldn't give you a sore throat or a hacking cough or lung cancer." - *(David Lodge, Nice Work. Viking, 1988)*
- "For we are all swimmers ephemerally buoyed by what will engulf us at the last; still dreaming of islands though the mainland has been lost; swept remorselessly out to sea while we spread our arms to the beautiful shore." *(Peter De Vries, Peckham's Marbles, 1986)*
- The new car's sexy design increased sales for the company.

- "Time is a dressmaker specializing in alterations." - *(Faith Baldwin, Face Toward the Spring, 1956)*
- "The streets were a furnace, the sun an executioner." - *(Cynthia Ozick, "Rosa")*
- "But my heart is a lonely hunter that hunts on a lonely hill." - *(William Sharp, "The Lonely Hunter")*
- Between the lower east side tenements, the sky is a snotty handkerchief." - *(Marge Piercy, "The Butt of Winter")*
- "I can mingle with the stars, and throw a party on Mars; I am a prisoner locked up behind Xanax bars." - *(Lil Wayne, "I Feel Like Dying")*
- "Love is an alchemist that can transmute poison into food--and a spaniel that prefers even punishment from one hand to caresses from another." - *(Charles Colton, Lacon)*
- "Men's words are bullets that their enemies take up and make use of against them." - *(George Savile, Maxims)*
- "A man may break a word with you, sir, and words are but wind." - *(William Shakespeare, The Comedy of Errors)*
- "The rain came down in long knitting needles." - *(Enid Bagnold, National Velvet)*
- "Language is a road map of a culture. It tells you where its people come from and where they are going." - *(Rita Mae Brown)*
- "I can mingle with the stars, and throw a party on Mars; I am a prisoner locked up behind Xanax bars." -- *(Lil Wayne, "I Feel Like Dying")*
- "Language is a road map of a culture. It tells you where its people come from and where they are going." -- *(Rita Mae Brown)*
- "Memory is a crazy woman that hoards colored rags and throws away food." -- *(Austin O'Malley, Keystones of Thought)*
- "Why this country is a shining city on a hill." -- *(Mario Cuomo, 1984 Democratic National Convention Address)*
- "With this faith we will be able to transform the jangling discords of our nation into a beautiful symphony of brotherhood." -- *(Martin Luther King, I Have a Dream)*

- "At the dawn of spring last year, a single act of terror brought forth the long, cold winter in our hearts. The people of Oklahoma City are mourning still." -- *(Al Gore, Oklahoma Bombing Memorial Address)*

CHAPTER FORTY-FIVE

Rhetorical Device 45 – Metonymy

Metonymy is a word or phrase which is used in place of another in the sentence, without changing its meaning or message. The substituted word or phrase is closely related to the replaced word and conveys its meaning. Such as "**crown**" for "royalty".

Another example-

"The **pen** is mightier than the **sword**," which originally came from Edward Bulwer Lytton's play Richelieu. This sentence has two examples of metonymy:

The "pen" stands in for "the written word"

The "sword" stands in for "military aggression and force"

Examples

- Ears - for giving attention (*"Lend me your **ears**!" from Mark Antony in Julius Caesar*)
- Eyes - for sight
- The library - for the staff or the books
- Pen - for the written word
- Sword - for military might
- Crown - in place of a royal person
- The White House - in place of the President or others who work there
- The Pentagon - to refer to the staff
- The restaurant - to refer to the staff

- Silver fox - for an attractive older man
- Hand - for help
- The name of a country - used in place of the government, economy, etc.
- The name of a church - used in place of its individual members
- The suits - in place of business people
- Dish - for an entire plate of food
- Cup - for a mug
- The name of a sports team - used in place of its individual members
- **The Pentagon** will be revealing the decision later on in the morning.
- **The restaurant** has been acting quite rude lately.
- We must wait to hear from **the crown** until we make any further decisions.
- **The White House** will be announcing the decision around noon today.
- If we do not fill out the forms properly, **the suits** will be after us shortly.
- **The United States** will be delivering the new product to us very soon.
- **The Yankees** have been throwing the ball really well, and they have been hitting better than they have been in the past few seasons.
- She's planning to serve **the dish** early in the evening.
- **The cup** is quite tasty.
- Learn how to use **your eyes** properly!
- **The library** has been very helpful to the students this morning.
- Can you please give me **a hand** carrying this box up the stairs?
- "Fear gives **wings**." -- *(Romanian proverb)*
- "**Detroit** is still hard at work on an SUV that runs on rain forest trees and panda blood." -- *(Conan O'Brien)*
- **The White House** asked the television networks for air time on Monday night.
- **The suits** on Wall Street walked off with most of our savings

- **"The B.L.T.** left without paying." -- *(Waitress referring to a customer)*

Rhetorical Device 46 -Onomatopoeia

Onomatopoeia is the use of imitative and naturally suggestive words, whose sound is very close to the sound they are meant to depict, for dramatic, poetic or rhetorical effect. These words suggest the source of sound that it describes which makes the description more suggestive and interesting. For example, 'Zip' or 'Murmur'.

Common occurrences of onomatopoeias include animal noises, such as "oink", "meow", "roar" or "chirp". Onomatopoeias are not the same across all languages; they conform to some extent to the broader linguistic system they are part of; hence the sound of a clock may be tick tock in English, dī dā in Mandarin, or katchin katchin in Japanese.

<u>Examples</u>

- **Cock-a-doodle-do**, crowed the rooster.
- The clock goes **ticktock**.
- The cow says **moo** all day long.
- With the **click** of a mouse I can open another window on my computer.
- The duck **quacked** at the bird.
- **Zip** up your pants.
- The birds like to **tweet** outside my window.
- Don't **belch** so loud.

- I was so cold my teeth were **chattering**.
- I heard the bees **buzzing**
- Everyone in the room **snapped** their fingers to the music.
- Don't **bump** your head on the door.
- The fireworks at the parade made a loud **boom**!
- **Poof**! The magician made the rabbit disappear.
- The pipes **rattled** in the basement.
- I heard the tires **schreech** as he tried to put on brakes.
- The fire **crackled** as it kept us warm from the fireplace.
- **Clap** your hands a little louder.
- Don't **bam** on that table again.
- If the dog **barks** again take him outside.
- Grandma loves to hear the **pitter-patter** of little feet around the house.
- I love to **splash** in the water.
- The **rustle** of the leaves reminds me March winds are here.
- **Hum** me an old favorite tune.
- **Ding** went the bell as it fell on the floor.
- Did your child **flush** the toilet?
- He let out a loud **whoop** at the graduation ceremony.
- **Ugh**, that cough syrup tastes nasty.
- I don't like it when a dog **growls** at me.
- **Ahem**. Could we have your attention please?
- Please **whisper** while you are in the library.
- Michelle likes to **slurp** her drinks.
- The **snort** of the hog was aweful.
- He can **neigh** just like a horse.
- He **mumbled** his words
- She **popped** the balloon with a pin
- The snakes **hissed** as we walked by the cage.
- She **moaned** and cried for a long time.
- The **ding dong** of the doorbell is not loud enough.
- We heard the **tlot-tlot** of the horses hoofs.
- I **squashed** the banana.

- **"Chug, chug, chug. Puff, puff, puff. Ding-dong, ding-dong**. The little train rumbled over the tracks." -- *("Watty Piper" [Arnold Munk], The Little Engine That Could)*
- **"Brrrrrrriiiiiiiiiiiiiiiiiiiinng!** An alarm clock clanged in the dark and silent room." -- *(Richard Wright, Native Son, 1940)*
- "I'm getting married in the morning! **Ding dong**! the bells are gonna chime." -- *(Lerner and Loewe, "Get Me to the Church on Time," My Fair Lady)*
- **"Plop, plop, fizz, fizz**, oh what a relief it is." -- *(Slogan of Alka Seltzer, U.S.)*
- **"Plink, plink, fizz, fizz"** -- *(Alka Seltzer, U.K.)*
- **"Klunk! Klick!** Every trip" -- *(U.K. promotion for seat belts)*
- "[Aredelia] found Starling in the warm laundry room, dozing against the slow **rump-rump** of a washing machine." -- *(Thomas Harris, Silence of the Lambs)*
- "He saw nothing and heard nothing but he could feel his heart pounding and then he heard the clack on stone and the leaping, dropping **clicks** of a small rock falling." -- *(Ernest Hemingway, For Whom the Bell Tolls)*

CHAPTER FORTY-SEVEN

Rhetorical Device 47 – Oxymoron

In Oxymoron the rhetorical impact is created by joining together two opposing ideas or contradictory words in a sentence or phrase. It gives a fresh meaning to the sentence as the contradictory placement of words evokes some measure of truth and conjures a new way of perception or understanding.

Some common examples of oxymoronic expressions are; act naturally, found missing, alone together, conspicuous absence, student teacher, deafening silence, definite possibility, definite maybe, terribly pleased, criminal justice, old news, peace force, even odds, awful good, random order, original copy, ill health, turn up missing, jumbo shrimp, loose tights, small crowd, and clearly misunderstood.

<u>Examples</u>

- "Hegel was right when he said that we learn from history that man can never learn anything from history." – *(George Bernard Shaw)*
- "I can resist anything, except temptation." – *(Oscar Wilde)*
- "Simplicity is not a simple thing." – *(Charles Chaplin)*
- "Always and never are two words you should always remember never to use." – *(Wendell Johnson)*
- "The best cure for insomnia is to get a lot of sleep." – *(W.C. Fields)*

- "Always be sincere, even when you don't mean it." – *(Irene Peter)*
- "If I could drop dead right now, I'd be the happiest man alive." – *(Samuel Goldwyn)*
- "The building was pretty ugly and a little big for its surroundings." – *(Steinbeck)*
- "The coldest winter I ever spent was a summer in San Francisco." – *(Mark Twain)*
- "To lead the people, walk behind them." – *(Lao-Tzu)*
- "I like a smuggler. He is the only honest thief." – *(Charles Lamb)*
- "And faith unfaithful kept him falsely true." – *(Alfred Tennyson)*
- "Modern dancing is so old fashioned." – *(Samuel Goldwyn)*
- "A business that makes nothing but money is a poor business." – *(Henry Ford)*
- "I am busy doing nothing." – *(Oxymorons)*
- "A little pain never hurt anyone." – *(Word Explorations)*
- "I am a deeply superficial person." – *(Andy Warhol)*
- "No one goes to that restaurant anymore - It's always too crowded." – *(Yogi Berra)*
- "We are not anticipating any emergencies." – *(Word Explorations)*
- "A joke is actually an extremely really serious issue." – *(Winston Churchill)*
- "I like humanity, but I loathe persons." – *(Edna St. Vincent Millay)*
- "Always be sincere, even though you do not necessarily mean it." – *(Irene Peter)*
- "I generally advise persons never ever to present assistance." – *(P.G. Wodehouse)*
- You know, this moment right here, it's -- it's **unbelievably believable**. You know, it's unbelievable because in the moment, we're all amazed when great things happen. But it's believable because, you know, great things don't happen without hard work. -- *(Robert Griffin III, 2011 Heisman Trophy Acceptance Address)*

CHAPTER FORTY-EIGHT

Rhetorical Device 48 – Paradox

Paradox occurs when a statement is self-contradictory or silly but contains some measure of truth. It generally contains two statements which are true mutually exclusive but are inappropriate simultaneously. But, together the sentence brings out a novel meaning or insight, which can be interpreted in a unique way, making the reader or listener think in an innovative, new or fresh way. This departure from the literal and straight- forward meaning is intentional with an objective of emphasis, clarity or novelty of expression.

Examples

- "If you wish to preserve your secret, wrap it up in frankness." -- *(Alexander Smith, "On the Writing of Essays." Dreamthorp, 1854)*
- "The close we are to danger, the farther we are from harm." -- *(Delivered by Billy Boyd from the movie The Lord of the Rights: The Two Towers)*
- "I have found the paradox, that if you love until it hurts, there can be no more hurt, only more love." -- *(Mother Teresa)*
- "Someday you will be old enough to start reading fairy tales again." -- *(C.S. Lewis to his godchild, Lucy Barfield, to whom he dedicated The Lion, the Witch and the Wardrobe)*
- "Mr. Chairman, Mr. President, my fellow Democrats, my fellow Americans: I proudly, and humbly accept your nomination." --

(Hubert Humphrey, 1964 Democratic National Convention Address)

<u>Examples of Paradox used in simple form:</u>

- The beginning of the end
- The person who wrote something so stupid can't write at all
- Men work together whether they work together or apart. – *(Robert Frost)*
- Be cruel to be kind
- Drowning in the fountain of eternal life
- Deep down, you're really shallow.
- Wise fool
- I'm a compulsive liar
- You can save money by spending it.
- I'm nobody.
- "What a pity that youth must be wasted on the young." – *(George Bernard Shaw)*
- If you didn't get this message, call me.
- Bittersweet
- A rich man is no richer than a poor man.
- Nobody goes to that restaurant because it is too crowded.
- You shouldn't go in the water until you know how to swim.

CHAPTER FORTY-NINE

Rhetorical Device 49 – Parallelism

Parallelism creates rhetorical impact in speech by adding lyrical flow in the delivery by giving two or more parts of the sentence a similar form, through recurrences of a word, phrase or clause, so as to give the passage a definite pattern. It uses the verbal components in the sentence which are grammatically identical, or similar in their construction, sound, meaning or meter. Its objective is to reinforce the message through introducing patterns in the sentence through repetitions.

For example - "People exercise **because they** want to look healthy, **because they** need to increase stamina, or **because they** hope to live longer."

<u>Examples</u>

- "...and that government **of the people, by the people, for the people,** shall not perish from the earth." -- *(Abraham Lincoln, Gettysburg Address here delivered by Jeff Daniels)*
- "For the Ireland of 1963, one of the youngest of nations and the oldest of civilizations, has discovered that the achievement of nationhood is not an end but a beginning. In the years since independence, you have undergone a new and peaceful revolution, an economic and industrial revolution, transforming the face of this land while still holding to the old spiritual and cultural values. You have **modernized your economy,**

harnessed your rivers, diversified your industry, liberalized your trade, electrified your farms, accelerated your rate of growth**, and improved the living standards of your people." -- *(John F. Kennedy, Address to the Irish Parliament)*

- **"We have petitioned and our petitions have been scorned. We have entreated and our entreaties have been disregarded.** We have begged and they have mocked when our calamity came. **We beg no longer. We entreat no more.** We petition no more. We defy them." -- *(William Jennings Bryan)*

- "Let every nation know, whether it wishes us well or ill, that we shall **pay any price, bear any burden, meet any hardship, support any friend, oppose any foe** to assure the survival and the success of liberty." -- *(John F. Kennedy, Inaugural Address)*

- "I've tried to offer leadership to the Democratic Party and the Nation. If, in my high moments, I have done some good, **offered some service, shed some light, healed some wounds, rekindled some hope,** or stirred someone from apathy and indifference, or in any way along the way helped somebody, then this campaign has not been in vain." -- *(Jesse Jackson, 1984 Democratic National Convention Address)*

- "We have seen the state of our Union in the endurance of rescuers, working past exhaustion. We've seen **the unfurling of flags, the lighting of candles, the giving of blood, the saying of prayers** -- in English, Hebrew, and Arabic." -- *(George W. Bush, 9-20-01 Address to the Nation on Terrorism)*

- Smith hopes to **visit his parents and see his old friends** when he goes home.

- She advised me to **find some new friends and forget about the event.**

- This wealthy car collector owns **three pastel Cadillacs, two gold Rolls Royces, and ten assorted Mercedes.**

- My brother **walks or rides** his bike to work.

- He ran up to the bookshelves, **grabbed a chair standing nearby, stepped painfully on his tiptoes, and pulled the fifty-pound volume on top of him, crushing his ribs and impressing him** with the power of knowledge.

- Peter drives **quickly and aggressively**.
- They don't mind **waiting and talking** while you get ready.
- **Quickly and happily**, he walked around the corner to buy the book.
- They want more time off in the **summer and on weekends**.
- **Each morning** we sing, **each morning** we dance, and **each morning** we pray.
- Before she leaves for work, she usually **eats breakfast and has a cup of coffee**.
- Sarah writes **poetry and short stories**.
- Peter felt that he had **made an excellent deal and that he had bought a masterpiece**.
- He enjoys **playing baseball and working out**.
- He left the engine on, **idling erratically and heating rapidly**.
- To think **accurately and to write precisely** are interrelated goals.
- "They had great skill in optics, and had instructed him to see **faults in others, and beauties in himself** that could be discovered by nobody else. . ." *(By Alexander Pope)*
- "For the end of a theoretical science is truth, but the end of a practical science is performance." *(By Aristotle)*
- "I say to you today, my friends, that in spite of the difficulties and frustrations of the moment I still have a dream. It is a dream deeply rooted in the American dream. **I have a dream** that one day this nation will rise up and live out the true meaning of its creed: "We hold these truths to be self-evident; that all men are created equal." **I have a dream** that one day on the red hills of Georgia the sons of former slaves and the sons of former slave-owners will be able to sit down together at the table of brotherhood. **I have a dream** that one day even the state of Mississippi, a desert state sweltering with the heat of injustice and oppression, will be transformed into an oasis of freedom and justice. **I have a dream** that my four little children will one day live in a nation where they will not be judged by the color of

their skin but by the content of their character. -- *(Martin Luther King Jr.)*

CHAPTER FIFTY

Rhetorical Device 50 - Parataxis

In Parataxis simple declarative phrases, clauses or sentences are placed independently together, generally without any conjunctive word or words. It put emphasis on a particular emotion, idea or setting by reinforcing the impression made by the previous one, creating a powerful overall impact. It can be contrasted with hypotaxis.

Examples

- "I came; I saw; I conquered." -- *(Julius Caesar)*
- "Dogs, undistinguishable in mire. Horses, scarcely better-- splashed to their very blinkers. Foot passengers, jostling one another's umbrellas, in a general infection of ill-temper, and losing their foothold at street corners." -- *(Charles Dickens, Bleak House, 1852-1853)*
- "In the bed of the river there were pebbles and boulders, dry and white in the sun, and the water was clear and swiftly moving and blue in the channels." -- *(Ernest Hemingway, A Farewell to Arms, 1929)*
- "I needed a drink, I needed a lot of life insurance, I needed a vacation, I needed a home in the country. What I had was a coat, a hat and a gun." -- *(Raymond Chandler, Farewell, My Lovely, 1940)*

- "I remember walking across 62nd Street one twilight that first spring, or the second spring, they were all alike for a while. I was late to meet someone but I stopped at Lexington Avenue and bought a peach and stood on the corner eating it and knew that I had come out of the West and reached the mirage. I could taste the peach and feel the soft air blowing from a subway grating on my legs and I could smell lilac and garbage and expensive perfume and I knew that it would cost something sooner or later . . .." -- *(Joan Didion, "Goodbye to All That." Slouching Towards Bethlehem, 1968)*
- "Twenty-two years old, weak, hot, frightened, not daring to acknowledge the fact that he didn't know who or what he was . . . with no past, no language, no tribe, no source, no address book, no comb, no pencil, no clock, no pocket handkerchief, no rug, no bed, no can opener, no faded postcard, no soap, no key, no tobacco pouch, no soiled underwear and nothing nothing nothing to do . . . he was sure of one thing only: the unchecked monstrosity of his hands." -- *(Toni Morrison, Sula, 1973)*
- We walked to the top of the hill, and we sat down.
- In the beginning God created the heaven and the earth. And the earth was without form and void; and darkness was upon the face of the deep. And the Spirit of God moved upon the face of the waters.
- The Starfish went into dry-dock, it got a barnacle treatment, it went back to work.

CHAPTER FIFTY-ONE

Rhetorical Device 51 - Parenthesis

Parenthesis is a descriptive phrase, clause, word or sentence which interrupts the normal progression of sentence to provide the extra information enclosed in commas, dashes or brackets, to make it more presentable and expressive.

There are three main types of brackets: round brackets - ( ), square brackets - [ ], and curly brackets - { }. They are used to mark off explanatory or qualifying remarks in writing. Parenthesis is also the insertion of some verbal unit that interrupts the normal syntactic flow of the sentence.

<u>Round Brackets - ( )</u>

Round brackets make for the most commonly used type of brackets. These brackets are also known as round brackets, open brackets or simply, brackets. Round brackets are used when the purpose is to try and include information that can otherwise be omitted.

<u>Examples</u>

- David (Tim's brother) fought like a lion because he had no choice but to.
- He started off his career by working as a journalist with Washington Post.
- Smith (Peterson's father) was quick to come to the rescue of his son.

- Ryan was not only an extremely good athlete but also a part of the International Olympic Committee (IOC).
- "The English (it must be owned) are rather a foul-mouthed nation." -- *(William Hazlitt, "On Criticism")*
- "It is now necessary to warn you that your concern for the reader must be pure: you must sympathize with the reader's plight (most readers are in trouble about half the time) but never seek to know the reader's wants. Your whole duty as a writer is to please and satisfy yourself, and the true writer always plays to an audience of one." -- *(William Strunk, Jr. and E.B. White, The Elements of Style. Allyn & Bacon, 1995)*
- "For the vagabond-voyeur (and for travelers voyeurism is irresistible), nothing is not for notice, nothing is banal, nothing is ordinary: not a rock, not the shoulder of a passer-by, not a teapot." -- *(Cynthia Ozick, "The Shock of Teapots")*
- "Get your facts first, and then you can distort them as much as you please. (Facts are stubborn, but statistics are more pliable.)" -- *(Mark Twain)*

Square Brackets - [ ]

Square brackets, also known as closed brackets or simply brackets are used when the purpose is to include information or material that was previously excluded by the original author. The use of square brackets can be noticed in quoted text. Square brackets can be used when a letter needs to be added to a word and also when a quote or sentence needs to be modified. Square brackets are even used when the purpose of translation needs to be met.

Examples

- He love[d] that he was asked to be a part of the preparations for her wedding.
- When the going gets tough, Anuja is the kind of person who pull[s] her socks and takes challenges head on.

- When you think you've had enough of one particular obsession, it would do you good to move on to a host of other obsession[s].
- X says: 'I love to eat burgers.' - She love[s] to eat burgers.
- X says: 'Although you are trying to hide from me, I know that you are in there, waiting for me to come and discover you.' - Although he tries to hide from her, she know[s] that he is in there, waiting for her to come and discover him.
- He was an expert at an ancient martial art [Kung Fu] that the country China is noted for.

Curly Brackets - { }

Curly brackets are mostly used in literature when a series of choices need to be made. These choices are put in curly brackets because they are equal or similar in nature. Curly brackets can also be noticed in musical notation where they are used to mark repetitions.

Examples

- Please choose amongst the soft drinks {Pepsi, Miranda, Appy, Thumbs-Up} and return to your respective places.
- Pick amongst the following {red shirt, pink shirt, white shirt, green shirt, yellow shirt} and leave the premises.
- "My very photogenic mother died in a freak accident (picnic, lightning) when I was three." -- *(Vladimir Nabokov, Lolita, 1955)*

CHAPTER FIFTY-TWO

Rhetorical Device 52 – Personification

Personification is a figure of speech in which things, animals, inanimate objects or abstract notions are defined to have human characteristics or attributes or are represented as possessing human form. To create rhetorical impact speakers and writers make an idea, object or thing to act and behave like human, for personifying it. Personification is utilized to create vivid pictures in the minds of the readers or listeners to connect them with the idea or object better.

Examples

- Justice is **blind** and, at times, **deaf.**
- **Money** is the only **friend** that I can count on.
- The **cactus saluted** any visitor brave enough to travel the scorched land.
- Jan ate the **hotdog** despite the **arguments** it posed to her digestive system.
- The **world** does not care to **hear** your sad stories.
- After **freedom's sweet kiss,** she could never return to the **doldrums of the factory.**
- Peggy heard the last piece of **cheesecake** in the refrigerator **calling** her name.
- The **sorry engine** wheezed its death cough.

- **Drugs dragged** him into this place and they wouldn't let him **leave** alive.
- The **buses** can be **impatient** around here.
- These **casinos** are always **hungry** enough to **eat** your dinner.
- He sang a **lonely song** to the **moonlight**.
- The candle **flame danced** in the dark.
- **Thunder grumbled** and **raindropsreported** for duty.
- The **moon** turned over to **face** the day.
- As fall turned to winter, the **trees** found themselves **wearing white**.
- The brown **grass** was **begging** for water.
- Our **society needs** strong leaders.
- One **unhappy icicle** wasted away in the day.
- The **sunflowers nodded** in the wind.
- Most **pianos** have pretty good **manners** but Stephan can make them sound rude.
- The traffic **noises argued** long into the night and finally Cal went to sleep.
- The **angry storm** pounded the tin shelter.
- A school of **rainbow** trout **swam** across the mouth of the river.
- The **silence crept** into the classroom.
- **Father Time** can always **catch up** to you, no matter how fast you run.
- This **city** never **sleeps**.
- The **sun** stretched its golden **arms** across the plains.
- My **heart** has been **skipping** around in my chest since I saw her.
- The **child** of **morning, rosy fingered dawn**, appeared.
- Any **trust** I had for him **walked** right out the door.
- And with those four words her **happiness died**.
- The **cigarettes stole** his health and spent it on phlegm.
- **Kiss** your **integrity** goodbye.
- The **trees** dropped their leaves and **rested**.
- I overheard the **streets talking** about you.
- Winter's **icy grip** squeezed his rib cage.
- The **business world** would **chew** you up and **spit** you out.

- The **clouds pushed** each other around in the sky.
- He had little to live for now that his **dreams** were **dead**.
- The **smell** of smoke **tattled** on the delinquent.
- The **wind whispered** the rumors of the forest.
- The jittery **hands of corruption orchestrated** the affairs at city hall.
- Still **waters shivered** in the wind.
- Those **greedy weeds** have **starved the petunias**.
- A case of **cupcakes** can be quite **charming** to an empty stomach.
- December **light** is brief and **uncharitable**.
- This **morning** had friendly **greetings** for peaceful sleepers.
- The **party died** as soon as she left.
- **Light** had **conquereddarkness**.
- "Oreo: **Milk's favorite cookie**." -- *(Slogan on a package of Oreo cookies)*
- "Only the champion daisy trees were serene. After all, they were part of a rain forest already two thousand years old and scheduled for eternity, so they ignored the men and continued to rock the diamondbacks that slept in their arms. It took the river to persuade them that indeed the world was altered." -- *(Toni Morrison, Tar Baby, 1981)*
- "The **road** isn't built that can make it **breathe hard**!" -- (Slogan for Chevrolet automobiles)
- "Unseen, in the background, **Fate was quietly slipping** the lead into the boxing gloves." -- *(P.G. Wodehouse, Very Good, Jeeves, 1930)*
- "Fear knocked on the door. Faith answered. There was no one there." -- *(Proverb quoted by Christopher Moltisanti, The Sopranos)*
- "Pimento eyes bulged in their olive sockets. Lying on a ring of onion, a **tomato slice exposed its seedy smile** ..." -- *(Toni Morrison, Love: A Novel. Alfred A. Knopf, 2003)*
- "Once again, the **heart of America** is heavy. The **spirit of America** weeps for a tragedy that denies the very meaning of our land." -- *(Lyndon Baines Johnson)*

- "I'm gonna speak to this mountain -- whether it's a **mountain of sickness**, whether it's a **mountain of debt**; whether it's a **mountain of loneliness**; whether it's a **mountain of despair** -- whatever this mountain is." -- *(T.D. Jakes, All I Have is a Seed on my Side)*

- "**Peace now celebrates** a great victory for the nations of Egypt and Israel and for all mankind." -- *(Menachem Begin, Camp David Peace Accords Press Conference, Sept. 1978)*

- "To the fans in Chicago, St. Louis and Atlanta, I wanna say 'thank you' for your support. Your chanting of 'B-r-u-u-u-c-e' as I entered the game always gave me chills. I wish I could trot out there and get that feeling again, but **Father Timehas caught up with me. First he took my arm**, then **he took my hair**, then **he took the color from my beard**. But **he cannot take the great friendships and memories I have from being a baseball player**." -- *(Bruce Sutter, Baseball Hall of Fame Induction Address)*

- "**Good morning, America**, how are you? Don't you know me I'm your native son. I'm the train they call the City of New Orleans; I'll be gone five hundred miles when the day is done." -- *(Steve Goodman, "The City of New Orleans," 1972)*

- "Today, we begin a new chapter in the history of Louisiana. I've said throughout the campaign that there are two entities that have the most to fear from us winning this election. One is **corruption** and the other is **incompetence. If you happen to see either of them, let them know the party is over**." -- *(Bobby Jindal, Louisiana Governor-Elect victory Speech)*

- "Such acts are commonly stimulated by forces of **hatred and malevolence such as today are eating their way into the bloodstream of American life**." -- *(USSC Justice Earl Warren, Eulogy for John F. Kennedy)*

- "The only monster here is the **gambling monster that has enslaved your mother! I call him Gamblor, and it's time to snatch your mother from his neon claws!**" -- *(Homer Simpson, The Simpsons)*

- "The operation is over. On the table, the **knife lies spent**, on its side, the bloody meal smear-dried upon its flanks. **The knife rests. "And waits."** -- *(Richard Selzer, "The Knife." Mortal Lessons: Notes on the Art of Surgery. Simon & Schuster, 1976)*
- "Dirk turned on the **car wipers, which grumbled** because they didn't have quite enough rain to wipe away, so he turned them off again. Rain quickly speckled the windscreen.
- "He turned on the wipers again, but they **still refused to feel** that the exercise was worthwhile, and **scraped and squeaked in protest."** -- *(Douglas Adams, The Long Dark Tea-Time of the Soul. William Heinemann, 1988)*

CHAPTER FIFTY-THREE

Rhetorical Device 53 – Pleonasm

Pleonasm is the use of extra word or words, which look repetitive and are not necessary, but bring clarity in the expression.

<u>Examples</u>

- burning fire
- cash money
- end result
- all together
- invited guests
- ATM machine
- HIV virus
- RAM memory
- absolutely necessary
- advance warning
- affirmative yes
- affluent rich
- CAD design
- cash money
- basic fundamentals
- circulated around
- classic tradition
- classify into groups
- climb up

- close proximity
- completely expired
- completely filled
- each and every
- eliminate altogether
- full satisfaction
- frozen ice
- hot fire
- little baby
- live witness
- more easier
- old customs
- old senior citizens
- past experience
- past history
- retreating back
- return back
- It's deja vu all over again. – *(Attributed to Yogi Berra)*
- "Smoking can kill you, and if you've been killed, you've lost a very important part of your life." – *(attributed to Brooke Shields)*
- Lead-lined coffins called a health risk.
- Census says rich have most of the money. *(news item)*
- Cliches are a dime a dozen–avoid them like the plague.
- Cure suggestibility with hypnosis.
- I've told you a million times, "Don't exaggerate!"
- Is that a mirage or am I seeing things?
- It's bad luck to be superstitious.
- I used to be an agnostic, but now I'm not so sure.
- Sometimes you can observe a lot just by watching. – *(Attributed to Yogi Berra)*
- Half the lies our opponents tell about us are not true.
- Football is an incredible game. Sometimes it's so incredible, it's unbelievable. -Tom Landry
- When large numbers of men are unable to find work, unemployment results. – *(Calvin Coolidge)*

- Anyone who goes to a psychiatrist ought to have his head examined. – *(Samuel Goldwyn)*
- I never make predictions, especially about the future. – *(Attributed to Samuel Goldwyn)*
- "In the city today, the temperature rose to 105 degrees. This sudden rise of temperature was responsible for the intolerable heat."
- "Trapped, like a trap in a trap." – *(Dorothy Parker)*
- I used to be indecisive, now I'm not sure.
- He lived his life to the end.
- Some people are superficial but that's just on the surface.
- The world is apathetic but I don't care.
- Treachery will often bring loyalty into question.
- Perspective is in the eye of the beholder.
- "If we do not succeed, we run the risk of failure." – *(attributed to former Vice-President Dan Quayle)*
- "The **most unkindest** cut of all." -- *(William Shakespeare, Julius Caesar)*

I forgot my PIN number for the **ATM machine**.

CHAPTER FIFTY-FOUR

Rhetorical Device 54 – Polysyndeton

Polysyndeton is the process of deliberately using series of conjunctions (and, or, but, for, nor, so, yet) or connecting words in close succession, when most of them could be replaced with a comma, for rhetorical effect by slowing the tempo or rhythm.

<u>Examples</u>

- They read **and** studied **and** wrote **and** drilled. I laughed **and** played **and** talked **and** flunked.
- "[I]t is respectable to have no illusions--**and** safe--**and** profitable--**and** dull." -- *(Joseph Conrad, Lord Jim, 1900)*
- "Most motor cars are conglomerations (this is a long word for bundles) of steel and wire **and** rubber **and** plastic, **and** electricity and oil **and** petrol **and** water, **and** the toffee papers you pushed down the crack in the back seat last Sunday." -- *(Ian Fleming, Chitty Chitty Bang Bang: The Magical Car, 1964)*
- "I don't care a fig for his sense of justice--I don't care a fig for the wretchedness of London; and if I were young, **and** beautiful, **and** clever, **and** brilliant, **and** of a noble position, like you, I should care still less." -- *(Henry James, The Princess Casamassima, 1886)*
- "In years gone by, there were in every community men and women who spoke the language of duty **and** morality **and** loyalty **and** obligation." -- *(William F. Buckley)*

- You wouldn't believe how many exams I've got. I've got semantics **and** pragmatics **and** sociolinguistics **and** psycholinguistics **and** syntax.
- "In years gone by, there were in every community men and women who spoke the language of duty **and** morality **and** loyalty **and** obligation." – *(From a speech by William F. Buckley)*
- "They all tasted to me like undersexed morons who had blundered **or** trickled into the wrong beds in automatic response to sexy advertisements, **or** to make themselves feel modern and emancipated, **or** to reassure themselves about their virility **or** their "normalcy," **or** even because they had nothing else to do." -- *(C.S. Lewis, The Screwtape Letters)*
- "We must change that deleterious environment of the 80's, that environment which was characterized by greed **and** hatred **and** selfishness **and** mega-mergers **and** debt overhang...." -- *(Barbara Jordan, 1992 Democratic National Convention Keynote Address)*
- "Oh, my piglets, we are the origins of war -- not history's forces, **nor** the times, **nor** justice, **nor** the lack of it, **nor** causes, **nor** religions, **nor** ideas, **nor** kinds of government -- not any other thing. We are the killers."
- "He pulled the blue plastic tarp off of him **and** folded it **and** carried it out to the grocery cart **and** packed it **and** came back with their plates **and** some cornmeal cakes in a plastic bag **and** a plastic bottle of syrup." -- *(Cormac McCarthy, The Road. Knopf, 2006)*
- We have ships **and** men **and** money **and** stores.
- He ran **and** jumped **and** laughed for joy.
- We lived **and** laughed **and** loved **and** left.
- You wouldn't believe how many exams I've got. I've got semantics **and** pragmatics **and** sociolinguistics **and** psycholinguistics **and** syntax.
- "It's got awesome security. And the right apps. It's got everything from Cocoa **and** the graphics **and** it's got core animation built in **and** it's got the audio **and** video that OSX is famous for. It's got all the stuff we want." – *(From Steve Jobs*

Keynote Address, Macworld 2007)
- "In years gone by, there were in every community men and women who spoke the language of duty and morality and loyalty and obligation." – *(From a speech by William F. Buckley)*
- We have ships **and** men **and** money **and** stores.
- He ran **and** jumped **and** laughed for joy.
- We lived **and** laughed **and** loved **and** left.
- They read **and** studied **and** wrote **and** drilled. I laughed **and** played **and** talked **and** flunked.

Rhetorical Device 55 – Procatalepsis

A speaker creates an impact by using procatalepsis when an objection or question is raised to his own arguments, ideas or opinions, in anticipation, and then immediately answering it to continue moving forward while directing his attention to arguments or points opposing either the thought process or its final conclusion. The objective of the speaker is to strengthen his delivery by dealing with expected opposing points before they are raised by his audience.

Examples

- This is a stupid question. Or is it? If we look closer we can find some important points here.
- So who needs ice removal in a warm climate? Well the night can get very cold. And of course when it's hot every day, you may want to head for the cooler hills!
- Of course you know this already, so why am I pointing it out? Well recent research has added new detail...
- "'I know what you're going to say.' (It was one of Grace's most irritating habits that she finished other people's sentences for them in a way that they had not intended.) 'That if they look at it properly they'll see that it wasn't our fault. But will they look at it properly? Of course they won't. You know what cats they are. They're only waiting for a chance. What I mean is that this

is just the chance they've been waiting for.'" -- *(Hugh Walpole, The Captives, 1920)*

- "I may be asked, why I am so anxious to bring this subject before the British public--why I do not confine my efforts to the United States? My answer is, first, that slavery is the common enemy of mankind, and all mankind should be made acquainted with its abominable character. My next answer is, that the slave is a man, and, as such, is entitled to your sympathy as a brother. All the feelings, all the susceptibilities, all the capacities, which you have, he has. He is a part of the human family." -- *(Frederick Douglass, "An Appeal to the British People." Reception speech at Finsbury Chapel, Moorfields, England, May 12, 1846)*

- "Someone will say: 'Yes, Socrates, but cannot you hold your tongue, and then you may go into a foreign city, and no one will interfere with you?' Now I have great difficulty in making you understand my answer to this. For if I tell you that this would be a disobedience to a divine command, and therefore that I cannot hold my tongue, you will not believe that I am serious; and if I say again that the greatest good of man is daily to converse about virtue, and all that concerning which you hear me examining myself and others, and that the life which is unexamined is not worth living--that you are still less likely to believe. And yet what I say is true, although a thing of which it is hard for me to persuade you." -- *(Plato, Apology, trans. by Benjamin Jowett)*

- "He knows every harbor, every cove and inlet throughout the chain; he has to." 'Those are fine credentials, Geoffrey, but hardly the sort--'

- "'Please,' interrupted Cooke. 'I haven't finished. To anticipate your objection, he's a retired officer of US Naval Intelligence. He's relatively young, early to mid-forties, I'd say, and I've no real knowledge of why he left the service, but I gather the circumstances weren't very pleasant. Still, he could be an asset on this assignment.'" -- *(Robert Ludlum, The Scorpio Illusion, 1993)*

- "No group in America has had as poor a start as the first Africans. You'll argue that other groups had to suffer indignities and even slavery, but I immediately remind you that they migrated (i.e. came by choice). Africans were wrenched (even if purchased) from their homeland, brutalized and forced to work for free." -- *(Nashieqa Washington, Why Do Black People Love Fried Chicken? And Other Questions You've Wondered But Didn't Dare Ask. Your Black Friend, 2006)*

CHAPTER FIFTY-SIX

Rhetorical Device 56 – Rhetorical Question

Rhetorical Question is used for forceful impact when a question is asked in order to make a point and without expectation of any answer. This deliberate question is utilized by the speaker or writer to divert their attention towards a specific message, assertion or viewpoint. Generally, the answer to the Rhetorical Question is either obvious or is immediately provided by the speaker or writer.

<u>Examples</u>

- "What the hell?"
- "It is near not a good place to visit. Is it?"
- "You are ashamed, aren't you?"
- "You were at the scene of the crime, correct?"
- "Are you kidding?"
- "You're not really going to wear that, are you?"
- "Are you stupid?"
- "You don't expect me to go along with that crazy scheme, do you?"
- "How much longer must our people endure this injustice?"
- "Can you do anything right?"
- "Why do I even bother?"
- "What shall we do with a drunken sailor?"
- "What defense to the homeless has, if the government will not protect them?"

- "How stupid is this new filing system we have?"
- "Are you sure?"
- "If your friend jumped off the bridge would you do it too?"
- "You don't think I'm that stupid, do you?"
- "Are you kids still awake?"
- "How did that idiot ever get elected?"
- "What business is it of yours?"
- "Aren't you ashamed of yourself?
- "Yeah, why not?"
- If you prick us, do we not bleed? If you tickle us, do we not laugh? If you poison us, do we not die? And if you wrong us, shall we not revenge? – *(From 'The Merchant of Venice' by Shakespeare)*
- "How do you solve a problem? Like Maria?"
- "How do you catch a cloud and pin it down?"
- "Marriage is a wonderful institution, but who would want to live in an institution?" -- *(H. L. Mencken)*
- "Aren't you glad you use Dial? Don't you wish everybody did?" -- *(1960s television advertisement for Dial soap)*
- "I forget, which day did God create all the fossils?" -- *(An anti-creationism bumper sticker, cited by Jack Bowen in If You Can Read This: The Philosophy of Bumper Stickers. Random House, 2010)*
- "Do you want to see the flower of the manhood of this country which has brought everlasting glory to our nation neglected in the hour of its greatest need and afraid to face temptation?" -- *(John D. Rockefeller, Jr.)*
- "The means are at hand to fulfill the age-old dream: poverty can be abolished. How long shall we ignore this under-developed nation in our midst? How long shall we look the other way while our fellow human beings suffer? How long" -- *(Michael Harrington, The Other America: Poverty in the United States, 1962)*
- "Must I argue the wrongfulness of slavery? Is that a question for republicans? Is it to be settled by the rules of logic and argumentation, as a matter beset with great difficulty, involving

a doubtful application of the principle of justice, hard to understand?" -- *(Frederick Douglass, "What to the Slave Is the Fourth of July?" July 5, 1852)*

- "Sir, at long last, have you left no sense of decency?" -- *(Joseph Welch, The Army-McCarthy Hearings)*
- "To actually see inside your ear canal--it would be fascinating, wouldn't it?" -- *(Letter from Sonus, a hearing-aid company, quoted in "Rhetorical Questions We'd Rather Not Answer," The New Yorker, March 24, 2003)*
- "If practice makes perfect, and no one's perfect, then why practice?" -- *(Billy Corgan)*
- "Isn't it a bit unnerving that doctors call what they do 'practice'?" -- *(George Carlin)*
- Can anyone look at the record of this Administration and say, "Well done"? Can anyone compare the state of our economy when the Carter Administration took office with where we are today and say, "Keep up the good work"? Can anyone look at our reduced standing in the world today and say, "Let's have four more years of this"? -- *(Ronald Reagan, 1980 Republican National Convention Acceptance Address)*
- "It really is time to ask ourselves, 'How can we allow the rich and powerful, not only to rip off people as consumers, but to continue to rip them off as taxpayers?'" -- *(Ralph Nader, 2000 NAACP Convention Address)*
- "But no one seems to mention morality as playing a part in the subject of sex. Is all of Judeo-Christian tradition wrong? Are we to believe that something so sacred can be looked upon as a purely physical thing with no potential for emotional and psychological harm? And isn't it the parents' right to give counsel and advice to keep their children from making mistakes that may affect their entire lives?" -- *(Ronald Reagan, Remarks to the National Association of Evangelicals, 1983)*

CHAPTER FIFTY-SEVEN

Rhetorical Device 57 – Scesis Onomaton

Scesis Onomaton is the technique of repetition to create rhetorical impact by using two or more different but synonymous words or phrases having nearly similar meaning, in the same sentence, to emphasize an idea.

Examples

- We succeeded, we were victorious, we accomplished the feat!
- Wendy lay there, motionless in a peaceful slumber, very still in the arms of sleep.
- May God arise, may his enemies be scattered, may his foes flee before him.
- A man faithful in **friendship, prudent in counsels, virtuous in conversation, gentle in communication, learned in all liberal sciences, eloquent in utterance, comely in gesture, an enemy to naughtiness, and a lover of all virtue and godliness.**
- "Let there be no illusions about the difficulty of forming this kind of a national community. It's **tough, difficult, not easy.** But a spirit of harmony will survive in America only if each of us remembers that we share a common destiny" -- *(Barbara Jordan, 1976 DNC Keynote Address)*
- For to us a Child is born, to us a Son is given, and the government will be on His shoulders. And He will be called **Wonderful Counselor, Mighty God, Everlasting Father, Prince of Peace.** --

(Mike Harper, KVNE Radio Tyler, TX)

- "Ah **sinful nation, a people laden with iniquity, a seed of evildoers, children that are corrupters.**"
- "But four years ago Jimmy Swaggart said this about me. He said, "This here song by The Police, 'Murder by Numbers', was written by **Satan,** performed by the Sons of Satan -- **Beelzebub, Lucifer, The Horned One.**" -- *(Sting - live with Frank Zappa in Concert)*
- "I'm a "leadership of the free world" duck. And I'm continuing to spread our agenda **globally, and around the world, as well as internationally.**" -- *(George W. Bush, 2006 White House Correspondents' Dinner)*
- "For whatever reasons, Ray, call it **fate; call it luck; call it karma.** I believe that everything happens for a reason." -- *(Delivered by Bill Murray from the movie Ghost Busters)*
- "Friends. Countrymen. Russians!" -- *(Delivered by Rade Serbedzija from the movie The Saint)*
- "There is no room in this country for any flag except our own. There is no room for the red flag. It is opposed to everything our government stands for. It stands for **anarchy, chaos, and ruin.** Smash it." -- *(Leonard Wood)*
- "Because he's the hero Gotham deserves, but not the one it needs right now. So, we'll hunt him...because he can take it...because he's not our hero. He's **a Silent Guardian, a Watchful Protector, a Dark Knight.**" -- *(Delivered by Gary Oldman from the movie The Dark Knight)*

CHAPTER FIFTY-EIGHT

Rhetorical Device 58 - Sententia

In Sententia the rhetorical impact is created by using an ancient, famous or popular maxim, proverb, saying, adages, aphorism or quotation to summarize the previous idea or argument. This method tends to add credibility to the argument as apparent wisdom implies 'truth'.

Examples

- You know what they say, 'Life is for living.' So let's get back to my place and do some real living!
- My father always told me that the wise man works smarter, not harder, which is why I think I need a break.
- 80% of knowledge is tacit, so no matter what I write, I cannot pass on all I know.
- "A man's as miserable as he thinks he is." -- *(Seneca the Younger)*
- "No man is laughable who laughs at himself." -- *(Seneca the Younger)*
- "Things forbidden have a secret charm." -- *(Tacitus)*
- "A bad peace is worse than war." -- *(Tacitus)*
- "Greater things are believed of those who are absent." -- *(Tacitus)*
- But, of course, to understand all is to forgive all.
- As the saying is, art is long and life is short.

- For as Pascal reminds us, "It is not good to have all your wants satisfied."
- "If you wish to be loved, love." -- *(Seneca the Younger)*
- "So, I'm happy tonight. I'm not worried about anything. I'm not fearing any man. **'Mine eyes have seen the glory of the coming of the Lord.'"** -- *(Martin Luther King, Jr., I've Been to the Mountaintop)*
- "The lesson we have to learn is that our dislike for certain persons does not give us any right to injure our fellow creatures. The social rule must be: **'Live and let live.'"** -- *(George Bernard Shaw)*
- "I am not a perfect servant. I am a public servant doing my best against the odds. As I develop and serve, be patient: **God is not finished with me yet."** -- *(Jesse Jackson, 1984 Democratic National Convention Address)*
- "We are now well into our fifth year since a policy was initiated with the avowed object and confident purpose of putting an end to slavery agitation. However, under the operation of that policy, that agitation has not only not ceased, but has constantly augmented. In my opinion, it will not cease until a crisis shall have been reached and passed. "**A house divided against itself cannot stand."** -- *(Abraham Lincoln, A House Divided Re-enactment delivered by Fritz Klein)*

CHAPTER FIFTY-NINE

Rhetorical Device 59 – Simile

Simile is a figure of speech comparing two different, dissimilar and unrelated things often introduced with the words like 'as', 'like' or 'than'. It is commonly in used in our daily speech like "he is slow as a snail". The objective of simile is to emphasize the point by using a common object, idea or thing which is known to the reader or listener.

Simile is similar to Metaphor as both are forms of comparison. Metaphors compare two things without using 'like', 'as' or 'than'.

Examples

- As large as life
- As cold as ice
- As common as dirt
- As cool as a cucumber
- As hard as nails
- As hot as hell
- As innocent as a lamp
- A light as a feather
- As tall as a giraffe
- As tough as nails
- As white as a ghost
- As sweet as sugar
- As sure as death and taxes

- As bold as brass
- As bright as a button
- As shiny as a new pin
- This contract is as solid as the ground we stand on.
- That guy is as nutty as a fruitcake.
- Don't just sit there like a bump on a log.
- That went over like a lead balloon.
- My love is like a red, red rose.
- You were as brave as a lion.
- They are as different as night and day.
- She is as thin as a toothpick.
- Last night, I slept like a log.
- He is as funny as a barrel of monkeys.
- This house is as clean as a whistle.
- He is as strong as an ox.
- Watching the show was like watching grass grow.
- That is as easy as shooting fish in a barrel.
- I am so thirsty, that my throat is as dry as a bone.
- This dress is perfect because it fits like a glove.
- They wore jeans, which made me stand out like a sore thumb.
- My love for you is a deep as the ocean.
- They fought like cats and dogs.
- "**He was like a cock** who thought the sun had risen to hear him crow." -- *(George Eliot, Adam Bede, 1859)*
- "**Human speech is like a cracked cauldron** on which we bang out tunes that make bears dance, when we want to move the stars to pity." -- *(Gustave Flaubert, Madame Bovary, 1856)*
- "**Good coffee is like friendship**: rich and warm and strong." -- *(Slogan of Pan-American Coffee Bureau)*
- "You know life, **life is rather like opening a tin of sardines.** We're all of us looking for the key." -- *(Alan Bennett, Beyond the Fringe, 1960)*
- "When Lee Mellon finished the apple he smacked his lips together like a **pair of cymbals.**" -- *(Richard Brautigan, A Confederate General From Big Sur, 1964)*

- "It is all, God help us, a matter of rocks. The **rocks shape life like hands around swelling dough**." -- *(Annie Dillard, "Life on the Rocks: The Galápagos")*
- "But **His strong love stands like a granite rock unmoved by the hurricanes of our inequity**." -- *(Originally delivered by Charles Haddon Spurgeon)*
- "If you are interested in becoming a TV journalist, it is a fine example of how not to do it. **I look like an exploding tomato and shout like a jet engine** and every time I see it [the video] makes me cringe." -- *(John Sweeney, "Row Over Scientology Video." BBC News, May 14, 2007)*
- "**Humanity**, let us say, **is like people packed in an automobile** which is traveling downhill without lights at terrific speed and driven by a four-year-old child. The signposts along the way are all marked 'Progress.'" -- *(Lord Dunsany)*
- "The Duke's **moustache** was rising and falling **like seaweed** on an ebb-tide." -- *(P.G. Wodehouse, Uncle Fred in the Springtime, 1939)*
- "The **living self** has one purpose only: to come into its own fullness of being, **as a tree comes into full blossom, or a bird into spring beauty, or a tiger into lustre**." -- *(D.H. Lawrence, "Each Man Shall Be Spontaneously Himself")*
- "**Life is like an onion**: You peel it off one layer at a time, and sometimes you weep." -- *(Carl Sandburg)*
- "The interior of the **Earth is rather like an onion**, made up of a series of concentric shells or layers." -- *(Martin Redfern, The Earth: A Very Short Introduction. Oxford Univ. Press, 2003)*
- "My **facelooks like a wedding-cake** left out in the rain." -- *(W.H. Auden)*
- "[H]e looked about as inconspicuous as a tarantula on a slice of angel food." -- *(Raymond Chandler, Farewell, My Lovely, 1940)*
- "The **plants** filled the place, a forest of them, with nasty meaty leaves and stalks **like the newly washed fingers of dead men**." -- *(Raymond Chandler, The Big Sleep, 1939)*

- "**Like a feather caught in a vortex**, Williams ran around the square of bases at the center of our beseeching screaming." -- *(John Updike, "Hub Fans Bid Kid Adieu," 1960)*
- "**My memory** is proglottidean, **like the tapeworm**, but unlike the tapeworm it has no head, it wanders in a maze, and any point may be the beginning or the end of its journey." -- *(Umberto Eco, "The Gorge")*
- "Matt Leinart slid into the draft like a bald tire on black ice." -- *(Rob Oller, Columbus Dispatch, Feb. 25, 2007)*
- " . . . Here comes, The white-haired thistle seed stumbling past through the branches, **Like a paper lantern** carried by a blind man." -- *(W.S. Merwin, "Sire." The Second Four Books of Poems. Copper Canyon Press, 1993)*
- "People in the streets see it now. They're running towards the East River -- thousands of them **dropping in like rats**. Now the smoke's spreading faster. It's reached Times Square. People are trying to run away from it, but it's no use. They're **falling like flies**." -- *(Delivered by Orson Wells from the original radio broadcast of War of the Worlds)*
- "She dealt with moral problems as a **cleaver deals with meat**." -- *(James Joyce, "The Boarding House")*
- "A **Republic whose history, like the path of the just**, is as the shining light that shineth more and more unto the perfect day." -- *(William Jennings Bryan)*
- "She has a **voice like a baritone sax** issuing from an oil drum, and hams even with her silences." -- *(John Simon, reviewing Kathleen Turner in Who's Afraid of Virginia Woolf? - April 2005)*
- "I've had some long nights in the stir. Alone in the dark with nothing but your thoughts, **time can draw out like a blade**. That was the longest night of my life." -- *(Delivered by Morgan Freeman from the movie The Shawshank Redemption)*
- "He's got a **face like a wet Sunday** in a debtors' prison." -- *(Joe Bennett, Mustn't Grumble. Simon & Schuster, 2006)*
- "It is a curious thing, the **death of a loved one**. It's **like walking up the stairs** to your bedroom in the dark and thinking that

there's one more stair than there is. Your foot falls down through the air and there's a sickly moment of dark surprise." -- *(Delivered by Jude Law from the movie A Series of Unfortunate Events)*

- "A **sickly light, like yellow tinfoil**, was slanting over the high walls into the jail yard." -- *(George Orwell, "A Hanging," 1931)*

Difference between Simile and Metaphor

- <u>Simile</u>: He is as stubborn as a mule. <u>Metaphor</u>: He is a mule.
- <u>Simile</u>: Your thoughts are like a storm. <u>Metaphor</u>: Your thoughts are a storm
- <u>Simile</u>: Your eyes are like sunshine. <u>Metaphor</u>: You are my sunshine.
- <u>Simile</u>: He eats like a pig. <u>Metaphor</u>: He is a pig.
- <u>Simile</u>: You are like a rock. <u>Metaphor</u>: You are a rock.
- <u>Simile</u>: The world is like a stage. <u>Metaphor</u>: The world is a stage.
- <u>Simile</u>: The noise is like music to my ears. <u>Metaphor</u>: The noise is music to my ears
- <u>Simile</u>: Her heart is like gold. <u>Metaphor</u>: Her heart is gold.
- <u>Simile</u>: You are as happy as a clown. <u>Metaphor</u>: You are a clown.

CHAPTER SIXTY

Rhetorical Device 60 - Symploce

Symploce is the simultaneous repetition of a word or phrase at the beginning and another at the end of successive clauses, lines or sentences. It is the combination of epistrophe and anaphora.

Examples

- "Let us let our own children know that we will stand against the forces of fear. **When there is talk of** hatred, **let us stand up and talk against it. When there is talk of** violence, **let us stand up and talk against it.**" -- *(William Jefferson Clinton, Oklahoma Bombing Memorial Prayer Service Address)*
- "**Against** yourself **you are calling him, against** the laws **you are calling him, against** the democratic constitution **you are calling him**" — *(Aeschines)*
- "Let England have its navigation and fleet—let Scotland have its navigation and fleet—let Wales have its navigation and fleet—let Ireland have its navigation and fleet—let those four of the constituent parts of the British empire be under four independent governments, and it is easy to perceive how soon they would each dwindle into comparative insignificance." -- *(The Federalist No. 4)*
- "**The yellow** fog that rubs its back upon the **window-panes, The yellow** smoke that rubs its muzzle on the **window-panes...**" -- *(T.S. Eliot, "The Love Song of J. Alfred Prufrock."Prufrock and*

Other Observations, 1917)

- "**The madman** is not the man who has lost **his reason. The madman** is the man who has lost everything except **his reason.**" -- *(G.K. Chesterton, Orthodoxy, 1908)*

- "Labour is the party of law and order in Britain today. **Tough on** crime and **tough on** the causes of crime." -- *(Tony Blair, speech at the annual Labour Party Conference, Sep. 30, 1993)*

- "**For wantof** a nail the shoe **was lost. For wantof** a shoe the horse **was lost. For wantof** a horse the rider **was lost. For wantof** a rider the battle **was lost. For want of** a battle the kingdom **was lost.** And all for the want of a horseshoe nail." -- *(Attributed to Benjamin Franklin and others)*

- "We remember today that all our gentle heroes of Vietnam have given us a lesson in something more: a lesson in living love -- **their love** for their families **lives; their love** for their buddies on the battlefields and friends back home **lives; their love** of their country **lives.**" -- *(Ronald Reagan, Address at the Vietnam Veterans' Memorial)*

- "**Much of what I say might sound** bitter, **but it's the truth. Much of what I say might sound** like it's stirring up trouble, **but it's the truth. Much of what I say might sound** like it is hate, **but it's the truth.**" -- *(Malcolm X)*

- "No one should dare to even think about being the Commander in Chief of this country if he doesn't believe with all his heart that our soldiers are liberators abroad and defenders of freedom at home. But don't waste your breath telling that to the leaders of my Party today...**They claimed** Carter's pacifism would lead to peace --**they were wrong. They claimed** Reagan's defense buildup would lead to war -- **they were wrong.**" -- *(Zell Miller, 2004 Republican National Convention Address)*

- "You don't want the truth because deep down in places you don't talk about at parties, **you** want **me on that wall -- you** need **me on that wall.**" -- *(Delivered by Jack Nicholson from the movie A Few Good Men)*

- "And while there will be time enough to debate our continuing differences, now is the time to recognize that **that which** unites **us** is greater than **that which** divides **us**." -- *(Al Gore, 2000 Concession Speech)*
- "My brother need not be idealized, or enlarged in death beyond what he was in life, to be remembered simply as a good and decent man, who **saw** wrong and tried to right **it**, **saw** suffering and tried to heal it, saw war and tried to stop **it**." -- *(Ted Kennedy, Eulogy for Robert F. Kennedy)*
- "We owe protection to those men first, and we owe the security for their families if they die. **I** say **it**! **I** voice **it**! **I** proclaim **it**! And **I** care not who in heaven or hell opposes **it**!" -- *(John Lewis)*

CHAPTER SIXTY-ONE

Rhetorical Device 61 – Synecdoche

It is a literary device which uses the part of something to refer to the whole (as 'hired hands' for 'workers') or vice versa (as 'the law' for 'police officers'). It can also use the general for specific (as 'thief' for 'pickpocket') or specific for general (as 'cutthroat' for 'assassin') or even the material for the things made from it (as 'steel' for 'sword').

<u>For Example</u>:

- The phrase "hired hands" can be used to refer to workmen.
- The word "head" refers to cattle.
- The word "wheels" refers to a vehicle.
- The word "bread" can be used to represent food in general or money (e.g. he is the breadwinner; music is my bread and butter).
- The word "sails" is often used to refer to a whole ship.
- The word "police" can be used to represent only one or a few police officers.
- The "pentagon" can refer to a few decision-making generals.
- "Capitol Hill" refers to both the U.S. Senate and the House of Representatives.
- At the Olympics, you will hear that the United States won a gold medal in an event. That actually means a team from the United States, not the country as a whole.

- If "the world" is not treating you well, that would not be the entire world but just a part of it that you've encountered.
- The word "society" is often used to refer to high society or the social elite.
- Referring to the United States as "America" when the "Americas" is actually made up of many countries.
- To refer to any carbonated beverage as "Coke".
- Facial tissue is often referred to as "Kleenex"
- The word "ivories" is often used to denote piano keys, even though the keys are no longer made of ivory.
- The word "lead" is commonly used to refer to bullets.
- Silverware or dishes made of silver may be called "silver" even if they aren't sold silver.
- The word "plastic" is commonly used to refer to credit cards.
- Using the word "barrel" for a barrel of oil or beer.
- A "keg" is used to refer to a keg of beer.

Other Examples

- Lend me your ears.
- It is sure hard to earn a dollar these days.
- The ship was lost with all hands. (sailors)
- IIis parents bought him a new set of wheels. (new car)
- He has many mouths to feed. (to look after many)
- White hair. (elderly people)
- All hands on deck
- There sits my animal guarding the door to the hen house.
- Give us our daily bread.
- He hurled the barbed weapon at the whale. (Harpoon)
- The little lady in Cleveland couldn't pay her heating bill.
- 9/11 tragedy.
- White-collar criminals.
- If I had some wheels I would put on a new thread and ask for Jenny's hand in marriage.

- "The rustler bragged he'd absconded with five hundred head of longhorns."
- "He shall think differently," the musketeer threatened, "When he feels the point of my steel."
- "The sputtering economy could make the difference if you're trying to get a deal on a new set of wheels." -- *(Al Vaughters, WIVB.com, Nov. 21, 2008)*
- All hands on deck.
- General Motors announced cutbacks.

CHAPTER SIXTY-TWO

Rhetorical Device 62 – Understatement

Understatement is used to reflect complimentary, humility, sarcasm or even derogatory tone by undervaluing the gravity of the statement. Understatement generally has the contrast between the reality and its description. It is an intentional effort by writer or speaker for restraint or to make a situation less important that it really is or to nullify the emphasis in expression.

Understatement is used when the writer or speaker wants to show politeness or modesty. It is also an excellent tool for sarcasm and usually has an ironic effect.

<u>Examples</u>

- "Okay. Successful test." - Just after annihilating a cleaning cart in 'Ghostbusters'.
- "You met me at a very strange time in my life."- In 'Fight Club'
- "Tickled" - When asked how his execution by firing squad went in 'Wolverine'.
- "This is gonna ruin my whole day." - After getting shot in 'Avatar'
- "It's a bit yellow" - while describing a very yellow canary.
- "You killed my family. And I don't like that kind of thing." - In 'The Chosen One'.
- "There is some music by Beethoven in his Ninth Symphony" - while describing Beethoven's famous work.

- "The food was tolerable" - on the food that was prepared by the best chef in the world.
- "The cars drove at a fair clip" - while watching a car race.
- "I know a little about running a company" - comment by a successful businessman.
- "The desert is sometimes dry and sandy" - While describing the driest desert in the world.
- "It is just a little cool today" - when the temperature outside is 5° below zero.
- "She's a little sensitive." - Describing Moaning Myrtle in 'Harry Potter and the Chamber of Secrets'.
- "There has been an incident on Praxis." - In 'Star Trek VI' on the destruction of Praxis.
- "It would appear someone objected to this union and wasn't able to hold their peace." - In 'Kill Bill' in response to the massacre at the bride's wedding.
- "I think we have slightly different opinions on this topic" - instead of saying "I don't agree with you at all.
- "It was ok" - when a top ranker was asked about his exam results.
- "I wouldn't say he was thin" - describing a very obese person.
- "He is a little on the old side" - describing a very old person.
- "I wouldn't say it tasted great" - on terrible food.
- "New York is not the cheapest place in the world" - instead of saying New York is expensive.
- "We have had a little rain" - when the entire area is flooded.
- "It's just a scratch" - when there is a huge dent.
- "Cannibalism is frowned upon in most societies." - In 'Charlie and the Chocolate Factory'
- "It's just a flesh wound." - In 'The Black Knight', after having both arms cut off, in 'Monty Python and the Holy Grail'
- "Well, that's cast rather a gloom over the evening, hasn't it?"- On being visited by the Grim Reaper in Monty Python's 'The Meaning of Life'
- "I have to have this operation. It isn't very serious. I have this tiny little tumor on the brain."

- *(Holden Caulfield in The Catcher In The Rye, by J. D. Salinger)*
- "Last week I saw a woman flayed, and you will hardly believe how much it altered her person for the worse."-- *(Jonathan Swift, A Tale of a Tub, 1704)*
- "This [double helix] structure has novel features which are of considerable biological interest." -- *(J. Watson and F. Crick)*
- "The grave's a fine and private place, But none, I think, do there embrace." -- *(Andrew Marvell, "To His Coy Mistress")*
- "I am just going outside and may be some time." -- *(Captain Lawrence Oates, Antarctic explorer, before walking out into a blizzard to face certain death, 1912)*

CHAPTER SIXTY-THREE

Rhetorical Device 63 – Zeugma

Zeugma is a figure of speech in which a word, usually a verb or an adjective applies to more than one noun blending together grammatically and logically different ideas. In simple words, two or more parts of a sentence are joined with common verb or noun.

For example, 'She lowered her standards by raising her glass, her courage, her eyes and his hopes.'In this sentence, the word "raising" applies to "her glass", "her courage", "her eyes" and "his hopes" and as a result, has a shocking effect.

<u>Examples</u>

- She gathered her wits and her knitting.
- He hid his feelings and the ball.
- She stayed his execution and at the hotel.
- He rang the bell and up her purchases.
- She batted her eyelashes and third.
- He played for keeps and money.
- He bought her story and a beer.
- She entered the data and his room.
- He fished for compliments and trout.
- He milked the situation and the cow.
- He flew the coop and the kite.
- He fell back on his sword and his position of power.
- He stole the show and my wallet.

- I grew alfalfa and bored.
- Do you have a cold, or a sister?
- "His boat and his dreams sank." (*Charles Dickens, I Love India*)
- His heart and his love fled away.
- "He opened his mind and his wallet at the movies."
- "She batted her eyelashes and third." (*Words & Stuff*)
- "He fished for compliments and for trout." (*Words & Stuff*)
- "I am leaving for greener pastures and 10 days." (*Charles Dickens, I Love India*)
- "First the door locked, then his jaw." (*Mesozeugma*)
- "Mr. Pickwick took his hat and his leave." (*Zeugma*)
- "The farmers in the valley grew potatoes, peanuts, and bored." (*Wunderland*)
- "She opened her door and her heart to the orphan." (*Wunderland*)
- She dug for gold and for praise.
- The disgruntled employee took his coat and his vacation.
- "He lost his coat and his temper." (*Zeugma*)
- "You held your breath and the door for me." (*Zeugma*)
- He held his temper and her hand.
- She made her breakfast and the bed.
- "The addict kicked the habit and then the bucket." (*Zeugma*)
- "She exhausted both her audience and her repertoire." (*Charles Dickens, I Love India*)
- "To wage war and peace." (*Charles Dickens, I Love India*)
- "She looked at the object with suspicion and a magnifying glass." (Charles Dickens, I Love India)
- "He milked the situation and the cow." (*Words & Stuff*)
- "She stayed his execution and at the hotel." (*Words & Stuff*)
- She looked at her the scene with her eyes and fear.
- "It was curtains for him and the window." (*Charles Dickens, I Love India*)
- "He held a high rank and an old notepad." (*Charles Dickens, I Love India*)

- He drowned his sorrows and his cat, but the relief was only temporary; it was only a matter of time before it took a more sophisticated victim to quell his disturbances.
- Her hopes drowned with it her belief in idealism, trust in heaven, certainty in goodness and purity of heart.
- She bought the 1994 election, an antique cereal bowl, and the farm.
- ". . . losing her heart or her necklace at the ball." *(By Alexander Pope)*
- "I fancy you were gone down to cultivate matrimony and your estate in the country", by Goldsmith.
- "Friends, Romans, countrymen, lend me your ears." *(By William Shakespeare)*
- It was fearful how he was neither an alien, nor a human walking on two legs, neither a creepy insect, nor a handsome apparition.
- He bit the bullet, his hand, and the dust.
- He threw a bomb and killed soldiers, maimed children, injured women and blinded men.
- "You are free to execute your laws, and your citizens, as you see fit." *(Star Trek: The Next Generation)*

About Authors

Nilam Pathak is a communication professional who has worked with global organizations and institutions to realize the potential of corporate employees, students and masses. She believes in the power of Personality Development and Communication Skills to empower the vulnerable.

She has trained professionals and trainers of various domains and nations. She is an internationally published author of eight books.

https://direct.me/nilam

Anshuman Sharma is an author and knowledge creator who has transformed the lives and work of people from every continent. His groundbreaking ideas in Thinking, Communication, Personality and Storytelling are revolutionary, simple and effective.

His belief in simplicity has created powerful solutions that can be used by everyone effortlessly.

Experience the free material from following links:

https://direct.me/anshuman